FRIEDRICH NIETZSCHE

FRIEDRICH NIETZSCHE

STATUE BY KLEIN

NIETZSCHE

AND OTHER EXPONENTS OF INDIVIDUALISM

BY

PAUL CARUS

Wipf & Stock
PUBLISHERS
Eugene, Oregon

Wipf and Stock Publishers
199 W 8th Ave, Suite 3
Eugene, OR 97401

Nietzsche and other Exponents of Individualism
By Carus, Paul
ISBN: 1-57910-685-4
Publication date 7/2/2001
Previously published by Open Court, 1914

TABLE OF CONTENTS

FRIEDRICH NIETZSCHE

ANTI-SCIENTIFIC TENDENCIES.

PHILOSOPHIES are world-conceptions presenting three main features: (1) A systematic comprehension of the knowledge of their age; (2) An emotional attitude toward the cosmos; and (3) A principle that will serve as a basis for rules of conduct. The first feature determines the worth of the several philosophical systems in the history of mankind, being the gist of that which will last, and giving them strength and backbone. The second one, however, appeals powerfully to the sentiments of those who are imbued with the same spirit and thus constitutes its immediate acceptability; while the ethics of a philosophy becomes the test by which its use and practicability can be measured.

The author's ideal has been to harmonize these three features by making the first the regulator of the second and a safe basis of the third. What we need is truth; our fundamental emotion must be truthfulness, and our ethics must be a living of the truth. Truth is not something that we can fashion according to our pleasure; it is not subjective; its very nature is objectivity. But we must render it subjective by a love of truth; we must make it our own, and by doing so our conduct in life will unfailingly adjust itself.

Former philosophies made the subjective element predominant, and thus every philosopher worked out a philosophy of his own, endeavoring to be individual and original. The aim of our own philosophy has been to reduce the subjective to its proper sphere, and to establish, in agreement with the scientific spirit of the age, a philosophy of objective validity.

It is a well known experience that the march of progress does not advance in a straight line but proceeds in epicycles. Man seems to tire of the rigor of truth. From time to time he wants fiction. A strict adherence to exact methods becomes monotonous to clever minds lacking the power of concentration, and they gladly hail vagaries. Truth, they claim, is relative, knowledge mere opinion, and poetry had better replace science. Then they say: Error, be thou our guide; Error, thou art a liberator from the tyranny of truth. Glory be to Error!

Similar retrograde movements take place from time to time in art. Classical taste changes with romantic tendencies. Goethe, Schiller and Lessing are followed by Schlegel and Tieck, Mozart and Beethoven by Wagner.

The last half-century has been an age of unprecedented progress in science and we would expect that with all the wonderful successes and triumphs of scientific invention this age of science ought to find its consummation in the adoption of a philosophy of science. But no! The mass of mankind is weary of science, and anti-scientific tendencies grow up like mushrooms, finding spokesmen in philosophers like William James and Henri Bergson who have the ear of large masses, proclaiming the superiority of subjectivism over objectivism, and the advantages of animal instinct over human reason.

These subjective philosophies if considered as expressions of sentiment, as sentimental attitudes toward the world, as poetical effusions of a semi-philosophical nature, are perfectly legitimate and can be indulged in as well as the several religions which in allegories attune the minds of their followers toward the All of which they are parts. There is no need to condemn arts or emotions for they have a right to exist just as they are.

We protest against subjectivism in philosophy only when it denies the possibility of an objective philosophy. We do not deny that the masses of the world are not, cannot be and never will be scientific thinkers. Science is the prerogative of the few, and the large masses of mankind will always be of a pragmatist type. If the pragmatist considered himself as a psychologist pure and simple showing how the majority of mankind argues, how people are influenced by their own interest and how their thoughts are warped by what they wish the facts to be, pragmatism would be a commendable branch of the science of the soul. Pragmatism explains the errors of philosophy and we can learn much from a consideration of its principles. It becomes objectionable only in so far as it claims to be philosophy in the strict sense of the word.

The name philosophy is used in two senses, first as we defined it above, as a world-conception based upon critically sifted knowledge; and secondly it is used in a vague general sense as wisdom in the practical affairs of life. And if pragmatism claims to be a philosophy in this second sense it ought not to deny that philosophy as a science is possible.

Philosophy as a science is philosophy *par excellence.* It is the only philosophy of objective validity. All other philosophies are effusions of subjective points of view, of attitudes, of sentiment. But we must insist that these two contrasts may exist side by side just as art does not render mathematics supererogatory, and as a physicist who in his profession devotes himself to a study of nature according to methods of an objective exactness may in his leisure hours paint a *Stimmungsbild* to give an artistic expression to a subjective mood.

This world is not merely the object of science. There are innumerable tendencies which exist and have a right to exist, but they ought not to banish science, scientific enquiry and scientific ideals from the place they hold; for science is the mariners' compass which guides us over the ocean of life, and though the majority of the passengers do not and need not worry about it, science is after all the only means which makes for progress and lifts mankind to higher and higher levels.

If we criticize men like James and Bergson and other philosophers of subjectivism we do it as a defence of the indispensable character of the objectivity of science as well as of philosophy as a science.

James and Bergson were by no means the originators of their method of philosophizing. There have been many sages before them who deemed the spectacles through which they viewed the world to be the most important or even the only significant issue of life's problems. The Ionian physicists were outdone by the sophists, and in modern times Friedrich Nietzsche expressed the most sovereign contempt for science.

Among all the philosophies of modern times there is perhaps none which in its inmost principle is more thoroughly opposed to our own than Nietzsche's, and yet there are some points of mutual contact which are well worth pointing out. The problem which is at the basis of Nietzsche's thought is the same as in our philosophy, but our solution is radically different from his.

Friedrich Nietzsche is a philosopher who astonishes his readers by the boldness with which he rebels against every tradition, tearing down the holiest and dearest things, preaching destruction of all rule, and looking with disdain upon the heap of ruins in which his revolutionary thoughts would leave the world.

For more than a century Germany has been the storm-center of philosophical thought. The commotions that started in the Fatherland reached other countries, France, England, and the United States, after they had lost their force at home. Kant's transcendentalism and Hegel's phenomenalism began to flourish among the English-speaking races after having become almost extinct in the home of their founders. Prof. R. M. Wenley of the University of Michigan, Ann Arbor, Mich., expresses this truth with his native Scotch wit in the statement which I do not hesitate to endorse, that "German professors when they die go to Oxford," and we may add that from Oxford they travel west to settle for a while in Concord, Boston, Washington, or other American cities.

Hegelianism had scarcely died out in the United States when Schopenhauer and Nietzsche began to become fashionable. The influence of the former has been felt in a quiet way for some time while the Nietzsche movement is of more recent date and also of a more violent character.

Nietzsche represents a type of most modern date. His was a genius after the heart of Lombroso. He was eccentric and atypical.

Lombroso's psychology is an outgrowth of nominalism which does not recognize an objective norm for truth, health, reason, or normality of any kind, and regards the *average* as the sole method of finding a norm. If, however, the average type is the standard of measurement, the unusually excellent specimens, being rare in number, must be classed together with all other deviations from the average, and thus a genius is regarded as abnormal as much as a criminal—a theory which has found many admirers in this age that is sicklied over with agnosticism, the modern offshoot of nominalism. The truth is that true genius (not the pseudo-genius of erratic minds, not the would-be genius of those who make a failure of life) is uncommonly normal—I had almost said "abnormally normal."

A perfect crystal is rare; so the perfectly normal man is an exception; yet for all that he is a better representative of the ideal of his type than the average.

Nietzsche was most assuredly very ingenious; he was unusually talented but he was not a genius in the full sense of the word. He was abnormal, titanic in his pretensions and aims, and erratic. Breaking down under the burden of his own thought, he ended his tragical career in an insane asylum.

The mental derangement of Nietzsche may be an unhappy accident but it appears to have come as the natural result of his philosophy. Nietzsche, by nature modest and tractable, almost submissive, was, as a thinker, too proud to submit to anything, even to truth. Schopenhauer had taught him that the intellect, with its comprehension of truth, is a mere slave of the will, *ancilla voluntatis*. Our cognition of the truth has a purpose; it must accommodate itself to our own interest. But the self is sovereign; the self wants to assert itself; the self alone has a right to exist; and the self that does not dare to be itself is a servile, menial creature. Therefore Nietzsche preaches the ethics of self-assertion and pride. He is too proud to recognize the duty of inquiry, the duty of adapting his mind to the world, or of recognizing the cosmic order of the universe as superior to his self. He feels bigger than the cosmos; he is himself; and he wants to be himself. His own self is sovereign; and if the world is not satisfied to submit to his will, the world may go to ruin. If the world breaks to pieces, it will only cause him to laugh; on the other hand, if his very self is forced to the wall in this conflict, he will still, from sheer pride, not suffer himself to abandon his principle of the absolute sovereignty of selfhood. He will not be a man, human and humane, but an overman *(Uebermensch)*, a superhuman despiser of humanity and humaneness. The multitudes are to him like cattle to be used, to be milked, fleeced and butchered, and Nietzsche calls them herds, animals of the flock, *Heerdentiere*.

Nietzsche's philosophy is unique in being throughout the expression of an emotion—the proud sentiment of a self-sufficient sovereignty of self. It rejects with disdain both the methods of the intellect, which submit the problems of life to an investigation, and the demands of morality, which recognize the existence of duty.

Other philosophers have claimed that rights imply duties and duties, rights. Nietzsche knows of rights only. Nietzsche claims that there is no objective science save by the permission of the sovereign self, nor is there any "ought," except for slaves and fools. He prides himself on being "the first Unmoralist," implying the absolute sovereignty of man—of the overman—and the foolishness as well as falsity of moral maxims.

DEUSSEN'S RECOLLECTIONS

PROFESSOR PAUL DEUSSEN, Sanskritist and philosopher of Kiel, was Friedrich Nietzsche's most intimate friend. They were chums together in school in Schulpforta, and remained friends to the end of Nietzsche's life. Nietzsche had come to Schulpforta in 1858, and Deussen entered the next year in the same class. Once Nietzsche, who as the senior of the class had to keep order among his fellow scholars during working periods and prevent them from making a disturbance, approached Deussen while he sat in his seat peacefully chewing the sandwich he had brought for his lunch and said, "Don't talk so loud to your crust!" using here the boys' slang term for a sandwich. These were the first words Nietzsche had spoken to Deussen, and Deussen says:[1] "I see Nietzsche still before me, how with the unsteady glance peculiar to extremely near-sighted people, his eye wandered over the rows of his classmates searching in vain for an excuse to interfere."

[1] See Dr. Paul Deussen's *Erinnerungen an Friedrich Nietzsche.* Leipsic, 1901.

FRIEDRICH NIETZSCHE

AS A PUPIL AT SCHULPFORTA IN THE YEAR 1861

Nietzsche and Deussen began to take walks together and soon became chums, probably on account of their common love for Anacreon, whose poems were interesting to both perhaps on account of the easy Greek in which they are written.

In those days the boys of Schulpforta addressed each other by the formal *Sie;* but one day when Deussen happened to be in the dormitory, he discovered in the trunk under his bed a little package of snuff; Nietzsche was present and each took a pinch. With this pinch they swore eternal brotherhood. They did not drink brotherhood as is the common German custom, but, as Deussen humorously says, they "snuffed it"; and from that time they called each other by the more intimate *du.* This friendship continued through life with only one interruption, and on Laetare Sunday in 1861, they stepped to the altar together and side by side received the blessing at their confirmation. On that day both were overcome by a feeling of holiness and ecstasy. Thus their friendship was sealed in Christ, and though it may seem strange of Nietzsche who was later a most iconoclastic atheist, a supernatural vision filled their young hearts for many weeks afterwards.

There was a third boy to join this friendship—a certain Meyer, a young, handsome and amiable youth distinguished by wit and the ability to draw excellent caricatures. But Meyer was in constant conflict with his teachers and generally in rebellion against the rules of the school. He had to leave school before he finished his course. Nietzsche and Deussen accompanied him to the gate and returned in great sorrow when he had disappeared on the highway. What has become of Meyer is not known. Deussen saw him five years later in his home at Oberdreis, but at that time he was broken in health and courage, disgruntled with God, the world and himself. Later he held a subordinate position in the custom house, and soon after that all trace of him was lost. Probably he died young.

This Meyer was attached to Nietzsche for other reasons than Deussen. While Deussen appreciated more the intellectuality and congeniality of his friend, Meyer seems to have been more attracted by his erratic and wayward tendencies and this for some time endeared him to Nietzsche. Thus it came to pass that the two broke with Deussen for a time.

The way of establishing a state of hostility in Schulpforta was to declare oneself "mad" at another, and to some extent this proved to be a good institution, for since the boys came in touch with each other daily and constantly in the school, those who could not agree would have easily come to blows had it not been for this tabu which made it a rule that they were not on speaking terms. This state of things lasted for six weeks, and was only broken by an incidental discussion in a Latin lesson, when Nietzsche proposed one of his highly improbable conjectures for a verse of Virgil. The discussion grew heated, and when the professor after a long Latin disquisition finally asked whether any one had something to say on the subject, Deussen rose and extemporized a Latin hexameter which ran thus:

"Nietzschius erravit, neque coniectura probanda est."

On account of the declared state of "mad"-ness, the debate was carried on through the teacher, addressing him each time with the phrase: "Tell Nietzsche," "Tell Deussen," "Tell Meyer," etc., but in the heat of the controversy they forgot to speak in the third person, and finally addressed their adversaries directly. This broke the spell of being "mad" and they came to an understanding and a definite reconciliation.

Nietzsche never had another friend with whom he became so intimate as with Deussen. Deussen says (page 9): "At that time we understood each other perfectly. In our lonely walks we discussed all possible subjects of religion, philosophy, poetry, art and music. Often our thoughts ran wild and when words failed us we would look into each other's eyes, and one would say to the other: 'We understand each other.' These words became a standing phrase which forthwith we decided to avoid as trivial, and we had to laugh when occasionally it escaped our lips in spite of us. The great ordeal of the final examination came. We had to pass first through our written tests. In German composition, on the 'advantages and dangers of wealth' Nietzsche passed with No. 1; also in a Latin exercise *de bello Punico primo;* but in mathematics he failed with the lowest mark, No. 4. This upset him and in fact he who was almost the most gifted of us all was compelled to withdraw."

While the two were strolling up and down in front of the schoolhouse, Nietzsche unburdened his grief to his friend, and Deussen tried to comfort him. "What difference does it make," said he, "if you pass badly, if only you pass at all? You are and will always be more gifted than all the rest of us, and will soon outstrip even me whom you now envy. You must increase but I must decrease."

The course of events was as Deussen had predicted, for Nietzsche though not passing with as much distinction as he may have deserved nevertheless received his diploma.

When Deussen with his wife visited Nietzsche in August 1907 at Sils-Maria, Nietzsche showed him a requiem which he had composed for his own funeral, and he added: "I do not believe that I will last much longer. I have reached the age at which my father died, and I fear that I shall fall a victim to the same disease as he." Though Deussen protested vigorously against this sad prediction and tried to cheer him up, Nietzsche indeed succumbed to his sad fate within two years.

* * *

Professor Deussen, though Nietzsche's most intimate friend, is by no means uncritical in judging his philosophy. It is true he cherishes the personal char-

FRIEDRICH NIETZSCHE

FROM PHOTOGRAPH IN THE POSSESSION OF PROFESSOR DEUSSEN

acter and the ideal tendencies of his old chum, but he is not blind to his faults. Deussen says of Nietzsche: "He was never a systematic philosopher. . . . The great problems of epistemology, of psychology, of esthetics and ethics are only tentatively touched upon in his writings. . . . There are many pearls of worth upon which he throws a brilliant side light, as it were in lightning flashes. . . . His overwhelming imagination is always busy. His thoughts were always presented in pleasant imagery and in language of dazzling brilliancy, but he lacked critical judgment and was not controlled by a consideration of reality. Therefore the creation of his pen was never in harmony with the actual world, and among the most valuable truths which he revealed with ingenious profundity there are bizarre and distorted notions stated as general rules although they are merely rare exceptions, as is also frequently the case in sensational novels. Thus Nietzsche produced a caricature of life which means no small danger for receptive and inexperienced minds. His readers can escape this danger only when they do what Nietzsche did not do, when they confront every thought of his step by step by the actual nature of things, and retain only what proves to be true under the touchstone of experience."

Between the negation of the will and its affirmation Nietzsche granted to Deussen while still living in Basel, that the ennoblement of the will should be man's aim. The affirmation of the will is the pagan ideal with the exception of Platonism. The negation of the will is the Christian ideal, and according to Nietzsche the ennoblement of the will is realized in his ideal of the overman. Deussen makes the comment that Nietzsche's notion of the overman is in truth the ideal of all mankind, whether this highest type of manhood be called Christ or overman; and we grant that such an ideal is traceable everywhere. It is called "Messiah" among the Jews; "hero" among the Greeks, "Christ" among the Christians, and *chiün,* the superior man, or to use Nietzsche's language, "the overman," among the Chinese; but the characteristics with which Nietzsche endows his overman are unfortunately mere brutal strength and an unscrupulous will to play the tyrant. Here Professor Deussen halts. It appears that he knew the peaceful character of his friend too well to take his ideal of the overman seriously.

We shall discuss Nietzsche's ideal of the overman more fully further down in a discussion of his most original thoughts, the typically Nietzschean ideas.

EXTREME NOMINALISM

ACCORDING to Nietzsche, the history of philosophy from Plato to his own time is a progress of the idea that objective truth (a conception of "the true world") is not only not attainable, but does not exist at all. He expresses this idea in his *Twilight of the Idols* (English edition, pp. 122-123) under the caption, "How the 'True World' Finally Became a Fable," which describes the successive stages as follows:

"1. The true world attainable by the wise, the pious, and the virtuous man,—he lives in it, he embodies it.

"(Oldest form of the idea, relatively rational, simple, and convincing. Transcription of the proposition, 'I, Plato, am the truth.')

"2. The true world unattainable at present, but promised to the wise, the pious, and the virtuous man (to the sinner who repents).

"(Progress of the idea: it becomes more refined, more insidious, more incomprehensible,—it becomes feminine, it becomes Christian.)

"3. The true world unattainable, undemonstrable, and unable to be promised; but even as conceived, a comfort, an obligation, and an imperative.

"(The old sun still, but shining only through mist and scepticism; the idea becomes sublime, pale, northerly, Koenigsbergian.)

"4. The true world—unattainable? At any rate unattained. And being unattained also unknown. Consequently also neither comforting, saving nor obligatory: what obligation could anything unknown lay upon us?

"(Gray morning. First dawning of reason. Cock-crowing of Positivism.)

"5. The 'true world'—an idea neither good for anything, nor even obligatory any longer,—an idea become useless and superfluous; consequently a refuted idea; let us do away with it!

"(Full day; breakfast; return of *bon sens* and cheerfulness; Plato blushing for shame; infernal noise of all free intellects.)

"6. We have done away with the true world: what world is left? perhaps the seeming? . . . But no! in doing away with the true, we have also done away with the seeming world!

"(Noon; the moment of the shortest shadow; end of the longest error; climax of mankind; *Incipit Zarathustra!*)"

The reader will ask, "What next?" Probably afternoon and evening, and then night. In the night presumably "the old sun," i. e., the idea of Plato's true world, which (according to Nietzsche) grew pale in the morning, will shine again.

Nietzsche's main desire was to live the real life and make his home not in an imaginary Utopia but in this actual world of ours. He reproached the philosophers as well as the religious leaders and ethical teachers for trying to make mankind believe that the real world is purely phenomenal, for replacing it by the world of thought which they called "the true world" or the world of truth. To Nietzsche the typical philosopher is Plato. He and all his followers are accused of hypocrisy for making people believe that "the true world" of their own fiction is real and that man's ambition should be to attain to this "true world" (the world of philosophy, of science, of art, of ethical ideals) built above the real world. Nietzsche means to shatter all the idols of the past, and he has come to the conclusion that even the scientists were guilty of the same fault as the philosophers. They erected a world of thought, of subjective conception from the materials of the real world, and so he denounces even their attempts at constructing a "true world" as either a self-mystification or a lie. It is as imaginary as the world of the priest. In order to lead a life worthy of the "overman," we should assert ourselves and feel no longer hampered by rules of conduct or canons of logic or by any consideration for truth.

With all his hatred of religion, Nietzsche was nevertheless an intensely religious character, and knowing that he could not clearly see a connection between his so-called "real world" and his actual surroundings, he developed all the symptoms of religious fanaticism which characterizes religious leaders of all ages. He indulged in a mystic ecstacy, preaching it as the essential feature of his philosophy, and his Dionysiac enthusiasm is not the least of the intoxicants which are contained in his thought and bring so many poetical and talented but immature minds under his control.

It is obvious that "the real world" of Nietzsche is more unreal than "the true world" of philosophy and of religion which he denounces as fictitious, but he was too naïve and philosophically crude to see this. Nietzsche's "real world" is a fabric of his own personal imagination, while the true world of science is at least a thought-construction of the world which pictures facts with objective exactness; it is controlled by experience and can be utilized in practical life; it is subject to criticism and its propositions are being constantly tested either to be refuted or verified. Nietzsche's "real world" is the hope (and perhaps not even a desirable hope) of a feverish brain whose action is influenced by a decadent body.

Nietzsche's so-called "real world" is one ideal among many others. It is as much subjective as the ideals of other mortals,—of men who seek happiness in wealth, or in pleasures, or in fame, or in scholarship, or in a religious life—all of them imagine that the world of their thoughts is real and the goal which they endeavor to reach is the only thing that possesses genuine worth. In Nietzsche's opinion all are dreamers catching at shadows, but the shadow of his own fancy appeared to him as real.

According to Nietzsche the universe is not a cosmos but a chaos. He says (*La Gaya Scienza*, German edition, p. 148):

"The astral order in which we live is an exception. This

order and the relative stability which is thereby caused, made the exception of exceptions possible,—the formation of organisms. The character-total of the world is into all eternity chaos, not in the sense of a missing necessity, but of missing order, articulation, form, beauty, wisdom, and as all our æsthetic humanities may be called."

In agreement with this conception of order, Nietzsche says of man, the rational animal:

"I fear that animals look upon man as a being of their own kind, which in a most dangerous way has lost the sound animal-sense,—as a lunatic animal, a laughing animal, a crying animal, a miserable animal." (*La Gaya Scienza*, German edition, p. 196.)

If reason is an aberration, the brute must be superior to man and instinct must range higher than logical thought. Man's reason, according to this consistent nominalist view, is purely subjective and has no prototype in the objective world. This is a feature common to all nominalistic philosophies. John Stuart Mill regards the theorems of logic and mathematics, not only not as truths, but as positive untruths. He says:

"The points, lines, circles, and squares, which any one has in his mind, are (I apprehend) simply copies of the points, lines, circles, and squares which he has known in his experience. Our idea of a point, I apprehend to be simply our idea of the *minimum visibile*, the smallest portion of surface which we can see. A line, as defined by geometers, is wholly inconceivable. We can reason about a line as if it had no breadth; because we have a power, which is the foundation of all the control we can exercise over the operations of our minds; the power, when a perception is present to our senses, or a conception to our intellects, of *attending* to a part only of that perception or conception, instead of the whole. But we cannot *conceive* a line without breadth; we can form no mental picture of such a line: all the lines which we have in our minds are lines possessing breadth."

Nietzsche shows his nominalistic tendencies by repeatedly pronouncing the same propositions in almost literally the same words,[1] without, however, acknowledging the school in which he picked up this error.

It is quite true that mathematical lines and circles are human conceptions, but they are not purely subjective conceptions, still less untruths; they are great and important discoveries. They are not arbitrarily devised but constructed according to the laws of the uniformities that dominate existence. They represent actual features of the factors which shape the objective universe, and thus only is it possible that the astronomer through the calculation of mathematical curves can predict the motion of the stars.[2]

Reason is the key to the universe, because it is the reflex of cosmic order, and the cosmic order, the intrinsic regularity and immanent harmony of the uniformities of nature, is not a subjective illusion but an objective reality.

When Goethe claims that all things transitory are

[1] *La Gaya Scienza,* German edition, p. 154; and *passim* in *Menschliches,* etc.

[2] For further details of a refutation of this wrong conception of geometry, see the author's *Foundation of Mathematics.*

symbols of that which is intransitory and eternal, Nietzsche answers that the idea of anything intransitory is a mere symbol, and God (the idea of anything eternal) a poet's lie.

Like a mocking-bird, the nominalist philosopher imitates the ring of Goethe's well-known lines at the conclusion of the second part of "Faust," in which the "real world" of transient things is considered as a mere symbol of the true world of eternal verities:

"Das Unvergängliche
Ist nur dein Gleichniss.
Gott der Verfängliche
Ist Dichter-Erschleichniss.
Weltspiel, das herrische,
Mischt Sein und Schein:—
Das Ewig-Närrische
Mischt uns—hinein."

"The non-deciduous
Is a symbol of *thy* sense,
God ever invidious,
A poetical license.
World-play domineeringly
Mixes semblance and fact,
And between them us sneeringly
The Ever-Foolish has packed."

In spite of Nietzsche's hunger for the realities of life, that is to say for objectivity, he was in fact the most subjective of all philosophers—so much so that he was incapable of formulating any thought as an objectively precise statement. He did not believe in truth: "There is probability, but no truth," says he in *Der Wanderer und sein Schatten,* p. 190; and he adds concerning the measure of the value of truth (*ibid.,* Aphorism 4): "The trouble in ascending mountains is no measure of their height, and should it be different in science?"

It is true that such words as "long" and "short" are relative, because dependent on subjective needs and valuations. But must we for that reason give up all hope of describing facts in objective terms? Are not meters and foot-measures definite magnitudes, whether or not they be *long* for one purpose and *short* for another? Relativity itself admits of a description in objective terms; but if a statement of facts in objective terms were impossible, the ideals of exact science (as all ideals) would be a dream.

That Nietzsche prefers the abrupt style of aphorisms to dispassionate inquisitions is a symptom that betrays the nature of his philosophy. His ideas, thus expressed, are easily understood. They are but very loosely connected, and we find them frequently contradictory. They are not presented in a logical, orderly way, but sound like reiterated challenges to battle. They are appeals to all wild impulses and a clamor for the right of self-assertion.

While Nietzsche's philosophy is in itself inconsistent and illogical, it is yet born of the logic of facts; it is the consistent result and legitimate conclusion of principles uttered centuries ago and which were slowly matured in the historical development of thought.

The old nominalistic school is the father of Nietzsche's philosophy. A consistent nominalist will be driven from one conclusion to another until he reaches the stage of Nietzsche, which is philosophical anarchism and extreme individualism.

The nominalist denies the reality of reason; he regards the existence of universals as a fiction, and looks upon the world as a heap of particulars. He loses sight of the unity of the world and forgets that form is a true feature of things. It is form and the sameness of the laws of form which makes universality of reason possible.

Nominalism rose in opposition to the medieval realism of the schoolmen who looked upon universals as real and concrete things, representing them as individual beings that existed *ante res, in rebus,* and *post res,* i. e., in the particulars, before them and after them. The realists were wrong in so far as they conceived universals as substances or distinct essences, as true realities (hence the name "realism"); only they were supposed to be of a more spiritual nature than material things but, after all, they were concrete existences. They were said to have been created by God as an artisan would make patterns or molds for the things which he proposes to produce. According to Plato, ideas serve the Creator as models of concrete objects of which they are deemed to be the prototypes. The realists were mistaken in regarding the ideal as concrete and real, but the nominalists, on the other hand, also went too far in denying the objective significance of universals and declaring that universals were mere names *(nomina* and *flatus vocis)*, i. e., words invented for the sake of conveniently thinking things and serving no other purpose.

At the bottom of the controversy lies the problem as to the nature of things. The question arises, What are things in themselves? Do things, or do they not, possess an independence of their own? Kant's reply is, that things in themselves can not be known; but our reply is, that the nature of a thing consists in its form; a thing is such as it is because it has a definite form. Therefore "things in themselves" do not exist; but there are "forms in themselves."

Form is not a non-entity but the most important feature of reality, and the pure laws of form are the determinative factors of the world. The sciences of the laws of pure form, logic, arithmetic, algebra, geometry, etc., are therefore the key to a comprehension of the world, and morality is the realization of ideals, i. e., of the conceptions of pure forms, which are higher, nobler, and better than those which have been actualized.

From our standpoint, evolution is a process in which the eternal laws of being manifest themselves in a series of regular transformations, reaching a point at which sentiency appears. And then evolution takes the shape of progress, that is to say, sentient beings develop mind; sentiments become sensations, i. e., representative images; and words denote the universals. Then reason originates as a reflex of the eternal laws of pure form. Human reason is deepened in a scientific world-conception, and becoming aware of the moral aspect of universality it broadens out into comprehensive sympathy with all forms of existence that like ourselves aspire after a fuller comprehension of existence.

Thus the personality of man is the reflex of that system of eternalities which sways the universe, and humanity is found to be a revelation of the core of the cosmos, an incarnation of Godhood. This revelation, however, is not closed. The appearance of the religions of good-will and mutual sympathy merely marks the beginning of a new era, and we may expect that the future of mankind will surpass the present, as much as the present surpasses savagery. Such is the higher humanity, the true "overman," representing a higher species of mankind, whom we expect.

Nietzsche's philosophy of "unmorality" looms on the horizon of human thought as a unique conception apparently ushered into this world without any preparation and without any precedent. It sets itself up against tradition. Schopenhauer, Nietzsche's immediate predecessor, regarded history as the desolate dream of mankind, and Nietzsche exhibits a remorseless contempt for everything that comes to us as a product of history. Nietzsche scorns not only law and order, church and state, but also reason, argument, and rule; he scorns consistency and logic which are regarded as toys for weaklings or as tools of the crafty.

Nietzsche is a nominalist with a vengeance. His philosophy is particularism carried to extremes. There is no unity of existence to him. The God-idea is dead —not only the old metaphysical notion of a God-individual, but also God in the sense of the ultimate ground of being, the supreme norm of the cosmos. Nietzsche's world is split up into particular selves. He does not ask how they originated; he only knows that they are here. Above all, he knows that his own self is here, and there is no bond of sympathy between it and other selves. The higher self is that which assumes dominion over the world. His ideal is brutal strength, his overman the tyrant who tramples under foot his fellowmen. Democracy is an abomination to him, and he despises the gospel of love as it is preached by both Christ and Buddha. This is the key to his anti-moralism and to the doctrine of the autonomy of selfhood.

Nietzsche's philosophy might be called philosophical nihilism, if he did not object to the word. He calls it positivism, but it is particularism, or rather an aristocratic individualism which in the domain of thought plays the same role that political nihilism plays in Russia. It would dethrone the hereditary Czar, the ruler by God's grace, but it would not establish a republic. It would set on the throne a ruthless demagogue, a self-made political boss—the overman. It is the philosophy of protest, and Nietzsche is conscious of being Slavic in thought and aspiration. Nor does he forget that his ancestors belonged to the nobility. He claims to have been descended from a Polish nobleman by the name of Niëtzki, a Protestant who came to Germany in the eighteenth century as a religious refugee.

Nietzsche's love of Slavism manifested itself in his childhood, for when the news of the fall of Sebastopol became known, Nietzsche, at that time a mere boy, was so dejected that he could not eat and gave expression to his chagrin in mournful strains of verse.

He who has faith in truth accepts truth as authority; he who accepts truth as authority recognizes duty; he who recognizes duty beholds a goal of life. He has found a purpose for which life appears worth living, and reaches out beyond the bounds of his narrow individuality into the limitless cosmos. He transcends himself, he grows in truth, he increases in power, he widens in his sympathies.

Here we touch upon the God problem. In defining God as the ultimate authority of conduct, we are confronted by the dilemma, Is there, or is there not a norm of morality, a standard of right and wrong, to which the self must submit? And this question is another version of the problem as to the existence of truth. Is there truth which we must heed, or is truth a fiction and is the self not bound to respect anything? We answer this question as to the existence of truth in the affirmative, Nietzsche in the negative.

But he who rejects truth cuts himself loose from the fountain-head of the waters of life. He may deify selfhood, but his own self will die of its self-apotheosis. His divinity is not a true God-incarnation, it is a mere assumption and the self-exaltation of a pretender.

Nietzsche's philosophy is more consistent than it appears on its face. Being the negation of the right of consistency, its lack of consistency is its most characteristic feature. If the intellect is truly, as Schopenhauer suggests, the servant of the will, then there is no authority in reason, and arguments have no strength. All quarrels are simply questions of power. Then, there is might, but not right; right is simply the *bon plaisir* of might. Then there is no good nor evil; good is that which I will, bad is that which threatens to thwart my will. Good and evil are distinctions invented for the enslavement of the masses, but the free man, the genius, the aristocrat, who craftily tramples the masses under foot, knows no difference. He is beyond good and evil.

This, indeed, is the consequence which Nietzsche boldly draws. It is a consistent anarchism; it is unmoralism, a courageous denial of ethical rule; and a proud aristocratism, the ruthless shout of triumph of the victor who hails the doctrine of the survival of the strongest and craftiest as a "joyful science."

Nietzsche would not refute the arguments of those

who differ from him; for refutation of other views does not befit a positive mind that posits its own truth. "What have I to do with refutations!" exclaims Nietzsche in the Preface to his *Genealogy of Morals*. The self is lord. There is no law for the lord, and so he denounces the ethics of Christianity as slave-morality, and preaches the lord-morality of the strong which is self-assertion.

Morality itself is denounced by Nietzsche as immoral. Morality is the result of evolution, and man's moral ideas are products of conditions climatic, social, economical, national, religious, and what not. Why should we submit to the tyranny of a rule which after all proves to be a relic of barbarism? Nietzsche rejects morality as incompatible with the sovereignty of selfhood, and, pronouncing our former judgment a superstition, he proposes "a transvaluation of all values." The self must be established as supreme ruler, and therefore all rules, maxims, principles, must go, for the very convictions of a man are mere chains that fetter the freedom of his soul.

A PHILOSOPHY OF ORIGINALITY

ONE might expect that Nietzsche, who glories in the triumph of the strong over the weak in the struggle for life, red in tooth and claw, would look up to Darwin as his master. But Nietzsche recognizes no master, and he emphasizes this by speaking in his poetry of Darwin as "this English joker," whose "mediocre reason" is accepted for philosophy.[1] To Nietzsche that which exists is the mere incidental product of blind forces. Instead of working for a development of the better from the best of the present, which is the method of nature, he shows his contempt for the human and all-too-human; he prophesies a deluge and hopes that from its floods the overman will emerge whose seal of superiority will be the strength of the conqueror that enables him to survive in the struggle for existence.

Nietzsche has looked deeply into the apparent chaos of life that according to Darwin is a ruthless struggle

[1] See Nietzsche's poems in the appendix to *A Genealogy of Morals*, Eng. ed., Macmillan, p. 248.

for survival. He avoids the mistake of those sentimentalists who believe that goody-goodyness can rule the world, who underrate the worth of courage and over-rate humility, and who would venture to establish peace on earth by grounding arms. He sees the differences that exist between all things, the antagonism that obtains everywhere, and preferring to play the part of the hammer, he showers expressions of contempt upon the anvil.

And Nietzsche's self-assertion is immediate and direct. He does not pause to consider what his self is, neither how it originated nor what will become of it. He takes it as it is and opposes it to the authority of other powers, the state, the church, and the traditions of the past. An investigation of the nature of the self might have dispelled the illusion of his self-glorification, but he never thinks of analysing its constitution. Bluntly and without any reflection or deliberation he claims the right of the sovereignty of self. He seems to forget that there are different selves, and that what we need most is a standard by which we can gauge their respective worth, and not an assertion of the rights of the self in general.

We do not intend to quarrel with Nietzsche's radicalism. Nor do we underrate the significance of the self. We, too, believe that every self has the liberty to choose its own position and may claim as many rights as it pleases provided it can maintain them. If it cannot maintain them it will be crushed; otherwise it may conquer its rivals and suppress counter-claims; but therefore the wise man looks before he leaps. Reckless self-assertion is the method of brute creation. Neither the lion nor the lamb meditate on their fate; they simply follow their instincts. They are carnivorous or herbivorous by nature through the actions of their ancestors. This is what Buddhists call the law of deeds or *Karma*. Man's karma leads higher. Man can meditate on his own fate, and he can discriminate. His self is a personality, i. e., a self-controlled commonwealth of motor ideas. Man does not blindly follow his impulses but establishes rules of action. He can thus abbreviate the struggle and avoid unnecessary friction; he can rise from brute violence to a self-contained and well-disciplined strength. Self-control (i. e., ethical guidance) is the characteristic feature of the true "overman"; but Nietzsche knows nothing of self-control; he would allow the self blindly to assert itself after the fashion of animal instincts.

Nietzsche is the philosopher of instinct. He spurns all logical order, even truth itself. He has a contempt for every one who learns from others, for he regards such a man as a slave to other people's thought. His ambition for originality is expressed in these four lines which he inserted as a motto to the second edition of *La Gaya Scienza:*

> "Ich wohne in meinem eignen Haus,
> Hab' niemandem nie nichts nachgemacht
> Und—lachte noch jeden Meister aus,
> Der nicht sich selber ausgelacht."

We translate faithfully, preserving even the ungrammatical use of the double negative, as follows:

> "In my own house do I reside,
> Did never no one imitate,
> And every master I deride,
> Save if himself he'd derogate."

We wonder that Nietzsche did not think of Goethe's little rhyme, which seems to suit his case exactly:

> "A fellow says: 'I own no school or college;
> No master lives whom I acknowledge;
> And pray don't entertain the thought
> That from the dead I e'er learned aught.'
> This, if I rightly understand,
> Means: 'I'm a fool by own command.'"

Nietzsche observes that the thoughts of most philosophers are secretly guided by instincts. He feels that all thought is at bottom a "will for power," and the will for truth has no right to exist except it serve the will for power. He reproaches philosophers for glorifying truth.

Fichte in his *Duties of the Scholar* says:

> "My life and my fate are nothing; but the results of my life are of great importance. I am a priest of Truth; I am in the service of Truth; I feel under obligation to do, to risk, and to suffer anything for truth."

Nietzsche declares that this is shallow. Will for truth, he says, should be called "will to make being thinkable." Here, it seems to us, Nietzsche simply replaces the word "truth" by one of its functions.

Truth is a systematic representation of reality, a comprehensive description of facts; the result being that "existence is made thinkable."

Nietzsche is in a certain sense right when he says that truth in itself is nothing; for every representation of reality must serve a purpose, otherwise it is superfluous and useless. And the purpose of truth is the furtherance of life. Nietzsche instinctively hits the right thing in saying that at the bottom of philosophy there is the will for power. In spite of our school-philosopher's vain declamations of "science for its own sake," genuine philosophy will never be anything else than a method for the acquisition of power. But this method is truth. Nietzsche errs when he declares that "the head is merely the intestine of the heart." The head endeavors to find out the truth, and the truth is not purely subjective. It is true that truth is of no use to a man unless he makes it his own; he must possess it; it must be part of himself, but he cannot create it. Truth cannot be made; it must be discovered. Since the scholar's specialized business is the elucidation of the method of discovering the truth—not its purpose, not its application in practical life—Fichte's ideal of the aim of scholarship remains justified.

Omit the ideal of truth in a philosophy, and it becomes an *ignis fatuus,* a will-o'-the-wisp, that will lead people astray. Truth makes existence thinkable, but thinkableness alone is not as yet a test of truth. The ultimate test of truth is its practical application. There is something wrong with a theory that does not work, and thus the self has a master, which is reality, the world in which it lives, with its laws and actualities. The subjective self must measure its worth by the objective standard of truth—to be obtained through exact inquiry and scientific investigation.

The will for power, in order to succeed, must be clarified by a methodical comprehension of facts and conditions. The contradictory impulses in one's own self must be systematized so that they will not collide and mutually annihilate themselves; and the comprehension of this orderly disposition is called reason.

Nietzsche is on the right track when he ridicules such ideals as "virtue for virtue's sake," and even "truth for truth's sake." Virtue and truth are for the sake of life. They have not their purpose in themselves, but their nature consists in serving the expansion and further growth of the human soul. This is a truth which we have always insisted upon and which becomes apparent when those people who speak of virtue for its own sake try to define virtue, or determine the ultimate standard of right and wrong, of goodness and badness. We say, that whatever enhances soul-growth, thus producing higher life and begetting a superior humanity, is good; while whatever cripples or retards those aspirations is bad. Further, truth is not holy in itself. It becomes holy in the measure that it serves man's holiest aspirations. We sometimes meet among scientists, and especially among philologists, men who with the ideal of "truth for truth's sake," pursue some very trivial investigations, such, for example, as the use of the accusative after certain prepositions in Greek, or how often Homer is guilty of a hiatus. They resemble Faust's famulus Wagner, whom Faust characterizes as a fool

> ". . . whose choice is
> To stick in shallow trash for ever more,
> Who digs with eager hand for buried ore,
> And when he finds an angle-worm rejoices."

Thus there are many trivial truths of no importance, the investigation of which serves no useful purpose. For instance, whether the correct pronunciation of the Greek letter η was *ee* or *ay* need not concern us much, and the philologist who devotes all his life and his best strength to its settlement is rather to be pitied than admired. Various truths are very different in value, for life and truth become holy according to their importance. All this granted, we need not, with Nietzsche, discard truth, reason, virtue, and all moral aspirations.

Nietzsche apparently is under the illusion that reason, systematic thought, moral discipline and self-control, are external powers, and in his love of liberty he objects to their authority. Did he ever consider that thought is not an external agent, but a clarification of man's instincts, and that discipline is, or at least in its purpose and final aim ought to be, self-regulation, so that our contradictory thoughts would not wage an internecine war? Thus, Nietzsche, the instinct-philosopher, appears as an ingenious boy whose very immaturity is regarded by himself as the highest blossom of his existence. Like an intoxicated youth, he revels in his irresponsibility and laughs at the man who has learned to take life seriously. Because the love of truth originates from instincts, Nietzsche treats it as a mere instinct, and nothing else. He forgets that in the evolution of man's soul all instincts develop into something higher than instinct, and the love of truth develops into systematic science.

Nietzsche never investigated what his own self consisted of. He never analyzed his individuality. Otherwise he would have learned that he received the most valuable part of his being from others, and that the bundle of instincts which he called his sovereign self was nothing but the heirloom of the ages that preceded him. In spite of his repudiation of any debt to others, he was but the continuation of others. But he boldly carried his individualism, if not to its logical conclusions, yet to its moral applications. When speaking of the Order of Assassins of the times of the Crusades, he said with enthusiasm: "The highest secret of their leaders was, 'Nothing is true, everything is allowed!'" And Nietzsche adds: "That indeed, was liberty of spirit; that dismissed even the belief in truth." The philosopher of instinct even regards the adherence to truth as slavery and the proclamation of truth as dogmatism.

THE OVERMAN

THE quintessence of Nietzsche's philosophy is the "overman." What is the overman?

The word *(Uebermensch)* comes from a good mint; it is of Goethe's coinage, and he used it in the sense of an awe-inspiring being, almost in the sense of *Unmensch,* to characterize Faust, the titanic man of high aims and undaunted courage,—the man who would not be moved in the presence of hell and pursued his aspirations in spite of the forbidding countenance of God and the ugly grin of Satan. But the same expression was used in its proper sense about two and a half millenniums ago in ancient China, where at the time of Lao-tze the term *chiün jen* (君人), "superior man," or *chiün tze,* "superior sage," was in common usage. But the overman or *chiün jen* of Lao-tze, of Confucius and other Chinese sages is not a man of power, not a Napoleon, not an unprincipled tyrant, not a self-seeker of domineering will, not a man whose ego and its welfare is his sole and exclusive aim, but a Christlike figure, who puts his self behind and thus makes his self—a nobler and better self—come to the front, who does not retaliate, but returns good for evil,[1] a man (as the Greek sage describes him) who would rather suffer wrong than commit wrong.[2]

This kind of higher man is the very opposite of Nietzsche's overman, and it is the spirit of this nobler conception of a higher humanity which furnishes the best ideas of all the religions of the world, of Lao-tze's Taoism, of Buddhism and of Christianity.

Alexander Tille, the English translator of Nietzsche's *Thus Spake Zarathustra,* translates the word *Uebermensch* by "beyond-man." But "beyond" means *jenseits;* and Nietzsche wrote *über,* i. e., superior to, over, or higher than, and the literal translation "overman" appears to be the best. It is certainly better than the barbaric combination of "superman" in which Latin and Saxon are mixed against one of the main rules for the construction of words. Say "superhuman" and "overman," but not "overhuman" or "superman." Emerson in a similar vein, when attempting to characterize that which is higher than the soul, invented the term "oversoul," and I can see no objection to the word "overman."

The overman is the higher man, the superhuman man of the future, a higher, nobler, more powerful, a better being than the present man! What a splendid

[1] *Lao-tze's Tao Teh King,* Chaps. 49 and 63.

[2] For a collection of Greek quotations on the ethics of returning good for evil, see *The Open Court,* Vol. XV, 1901, pp. 9-12.

idea! Since evolution has been accepted as a truth, we may fairly trust that we all believe in the overman. All our reformers believe in the possibility of realizing a higher mankind. We Americans especially have faith in the coming of the kingdom of the overman, and our endeavor is concentrated in hastening his arrival. The question is only, What is the overman and how can we make this ideal of a higher development actual?

Happy Nietzsche! You need not trouble yourself about consistency; you reject all ideals as superstitions, and then introduce an ideal of your own. "There you see," says an admirer of Nietzsche, "what a splendid principle it is not to own any allegiance to logic, or rule, or consistency. The best thought of Nietzsche's would never have been uttered if he had remained faithful to his own principles."

However ingenious the idea of an overman may be, Nietzsche carries his propositions to such extremes that in spite of many flashes of truth they become in the end ridiculous and even absurd. His ideal is good, but he utterly fails to comprehend its nature and also the mode in which alone the overman can be realized.

Nietzsche proclaims the coming of the "overman," but his overman is not superior by intellect, wisdom, or nobility of character, but by vigor, by strength, by an unbending desire for power and an unscrupulous determination. The blond barbarian of the north who tramples under foot the citizens of Greece and Rome,

Napoleon I, and the Assyrian conqueror,—such are his heroes in whom this higher manhood formerly manifested itself.

He saw in the history of human thought, the development of the notion of the "true world," which to him was a mere subjective phantom, a superstition; but a reaction must set in, and he prophesied that the doom of nihilism would sweep over the civilized world applying the torch to its temples, churches and institutions. Upon the ruins of the old world the real man, the overman, would rise and establish his own empire, an empire of unlimited power in which the herds, i. e., the common people, would become subservient. The "herd animal" (so Nietzsche called any one foolish enough to recognize morality and truth) is born to obey. He is destined to be trodden under foot by the overman who is strong and also unscrupulous enough to use the herds and govern them.

Nietzsche was by no means under the illusion that the rule of the overman would be lasting, but he took comfort in the thought that though there would be periods in which the slaves would assert themselves and establish an era of the herd animals, the overman would nevertheless assert himself from time to time, and this was what he called his "doctrine of the eternal return"—the gospel of his philosophy. The highest summit of existence is reached in those phases of the denouement of human life when the overman has full control over the herds which are driven into the field, sheared and butchered for the sole benefit of him who knows the secret that this world has no moral significance beyond being a prey to his good pleasure. Nietzsche's hope is certainly not desirable for the mass of mankind, but even the fate of the overman himself would appear as little enviable a condition as that of the tyrant Dionysius under the sword of Damocles, or the Czar of Russia living in constant fear of the anarchistic bomb.

Nietzsche, feeling that his thoughts were untimely, lived in the hope of "the coming of the great day" on which his views would find recognition. He looked upon the present as a rebellion against the spirit of strength and vigor; Christianity especially, and its doctrine of humility and love for the down-trodden was hateful to him. He speaks of it as a rebellion of slaves and places in the same category the democraticism that now characterizes the tendency of human development which he denounces as a pseudo-civilization.

He insists that the overman is beyond good and evil; and yet it is obvious that though he claims to be the first philosopher who maintained the principle of unmorality, he was only the first philosopher boldly to proclaim it. His maxim (or lack of maxims) has been stealthily and secretly in use among all those classes whom he calls "overmen," great and small. The great overmen are conquerors and tyrants, who meteorlike appear and disappear, the small ones are commonly characterized as the criminal classes; but there is this difference between the two, that the former, at least so far as they have succeeded, recognize the absolute necessity of establishing law and order, and though they may temporarily have infringed upon the rules of morality themselves, they have finally come always to the conclusion that in order to maintain their position they must enforce upon others the usual rules of morality.

Both Alexander and Cæsar were magnanimous at the right moment. They showed mercy to the vanquished, they exercised justice frequently against their own personal likes or dislikes, and were by no means men of impulse as Nietzsche would have his overman be. The same is true of Napoleon whose success is mainly due to making himself subservient to the needs of his age. As soon as he assumed the highest power in France, Napoleon replaced the frivolous tone at his court, to which his first wife Josephine had been accustomed, by an observance of so-called *bourgeois* decency, and he enforced it against her inclinations and his own.

Further, Napoleon served the interests of Germany more than is commonly acknowledged by sweeping out of existence the mediæval system of innumerable sovereigns, ecclesiastical as well as secular, who in conformity with the conservative tenor of the German people had irremediably ensconced themselves in their hereditary rights to the disadvantage of the people. Moreover, the *Code Napoleon*, the new law book, perhaps the most enduring work of Napoleon, was compiled by the jurists of the time, not because Napoleon cared for justice, but because he saw that the only way of establishing a stable government was by acknowledging rules of equity and by enforcing their recognition. It is true that Napoleon made his service in the cause of right and justice a pedestal for himself, but in contrast to Nietzsche's ideas we must notice that this recognition of principle was the only way of success to a man whose natural tendency was an unbounded egotism, an unlimited desire for power.

In spite of his enthusiasm in announcing the advent of an overman, Nietzsche would be a poor adviser for a rising usurper. He would be able to cause a great upheaval, to bring about a Volcanic eruption, or to raise a thunderstorm wherever restlessness prevails, but his philosophy lacks the principle of using discretion, or advising self-discipline, of applying scientific methods—all of which is indispensable for success. He preaches boldness, not wisdom; and a hero after Nietzsche's heart would be like a navigator who courageously ventures into the storm but scorns a chart and leaves the mariners' compass behind; he would steer not as circumstances demand but according to his own sweet will, and would be wrecked before ever reaching the harbor of overmanhood.

How much greater is the ideal of the overman as taught by the ancient philosopher of China! He, the *chiün jen,* the superior man, does not need power either political or financial to be great; he does not need a pedestal of oppressed slaves to stand on; he is great in himself, because he has a great compassionate heart and a broad comprehensive mind. He is simple, and, as we read in the *Tao Teh King,* "He wears wool [is not dressed in silk and purple] and wears his jewel concealed in his bosom."

ZARATHUSTRA

TO those who have not the time to wade through the twelve volumes of Nietzsche's works and yet wish to become acquainted with him at his best, we recommend a perusal of his book *Thus Spake Zarathustra.* It is original and interesting, full of striking passages, sometimes flashes with deep truths, then again is sterile and unprofitable, or even tedious, and sometimes absurd; but at any rate it presents the embodiment of Nietzsche's grandest thoughts in their most attractive and characteristic form. We need scarcely warn the reader that Zarathustra is only another name for Friedrich Nietzsche and has nothing to do with the historical person of that name, the great Iranian prophet, the founder of Mazdaism.

Nietzche's Zarathustra is a hermit philosopher who, weary of his wisdom, leaves his cave and comes to mingle with men, to teach them the overman. He meets a saint who loves God, and Zarathustra leaving him says: "Is it possible? This old saint in his forest has not yet heard that God is dead!"

FRIEDRICH NIETZSCHE

IN THE PRIME OF LIFE

Zarathustra preaches to a crowd in the market:

"I teach you the overman. Man is a something that shall be surpassed. What have ye done to surpass him?

"All beings hitherto have created something beyond themselves: and are ye going to be the ebb of this great tide and rather revert to the animal than surpass man?

"What with man is the ape? A joke or a sore shame. Man shall be the same for the overman, a joke or a sore shame.

"Behold, I teach you the overman!

"The overman is the significance of the earth. Your will shall say; the overman shall be the significance of the earth.

"I conjure you, my brethren, remain faithful to the earth and do not believe those who speak unto you of superterrestrial hopes! Poisoners they are whether they know it or not.

"Verily, a muddy stream is man. One must be the ocean to be able to receive a muddy stream without becoming unclean.

"Behold, I teach you the overman: he is that ocean, in him your great contempt can sink.

"What is the greatest thing ye can experience? That is the hour of great contempt. The hour in which not only your happiness, but your reason and virtue as well, turn loathsome.

"I love him who is of a free spirit and of a free heart: thus his head is merely the intestine of his heart, but his heart driveth him to destruction.

"I love all those who are like heavy drops falling one by one from the dark cloud lowering over men: they announce the coming of the lightning and perish in the announcing.

"Behold, I am an announcer of the lightning and a heavy drop from the clouds; that lightning's name is the overman."

Zarathustra comes as an enemy of the good and the just. He says:

"Lo, the good and just! Whom do they hate most? Him who breaketh to pieces their tables of values,—the law-breaker, the criminal:—but he is the creator.

"The destroyer of morality I am called by the good and just: my tale is immoral."

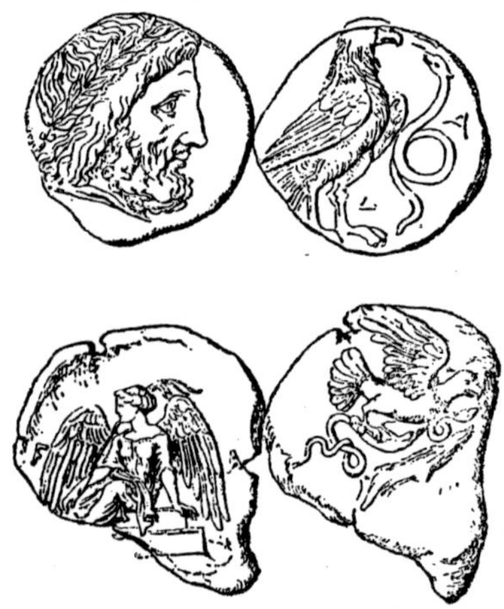

Coins of Ancient Elis.

Each is worth two drachmæ. One shows on the obverse a Zeus head with a laurel wreath, the other a winged Victory.

Nietzsche's favorite animals are the proud eagle and the cunning serpent, the former because it typifies aristocracy, the latter as the wisest among all creatures of the earth. It is a strange and exceptional combination, for these two animals are commonly represented as enemies. The eagle and serpent was the emblem of ancient Elis and is at present the coat-of-arms of Mexico, but in both cases the eagle is interpreted to be the conqueror of the serpent, not its friend, carrying it as his prey in his claws.

Zarathustra's philosophy is a combination of the eagle's pride and the serpent's wisdom, which Nietzsche describes thus:

"Lo! an eagle swept through the air in wide circles, a serpent hanging from it not like a prey, but like a friend: coiling round its neck.

"'They are mine animals,' said Zarathustra and rejoiced heartily.

"The proudest animal under the sun, and the wisest animal under the sun have set out to reconnoitre.

"They wish to learn whether Zarathustra still liveth. Verily, do I still live.

"More dangerous than among animals I found it among men. Dangerous ways are taken by Zarathustra. Let mine animals lead me!"

Here is a sentence worth quoting:

"Of all that is written I love only that which the writer wrote with his blood. Write with blood, and thou wilt learn that blood is spirit."

In another chapter on the back-worlds-men Nietzsche writes:

"Once Zarathustra threw his spell beyond man, like all back-worlds-men. Then the world seemed to me the work of a suffering and tortured God.

"Alas! brethren, that God whom I created was man's work and man's madness, like all Gods!

"Man he was, and but a poor piece of man and the I.

From mine own ashes and flame it came unto me, that ghost, yea verily! It did not come unto me from beyond!

"What happened, brethren? I overcame myself, the sufferer, and carrying mine own ashes unto the mountains invented for myself a brighter flame. And lo! the ghost departed from me!

"Now to me, the convalescent, it would be suffering and pain to believe in such ghosts: suffering it would be for me and humiliation. Thus spake I unto the back-worlds-men."

Nietzsche's self is not ideal but material; it is not thought, not even the will, but the body. The following passage sounds like Vedantism as interpreted by a materialist:

"He who is awake and knoweth saith: Body I am throughout, and nothing besides; and soul is merely a word for a something in body.

"Body is one great reason, a plurality with one sense, a war and a peace, a flock and a herdsman.

"Also thy little reason, my brother, which thou callest 'spirit'—it is a tool of thy body, a little tool and toy of thy great reason.

" 'I', thou sayest and art proud of that word. But the greater thing is—which thou wilt not believe—thy body and its great reason. It doth not say 'I', but it is the acting 'I.'

"The self ever listeneth and seeketh: it compareth, subdueth, conquereth, destroyeth. It ruleth and is the ruler of the 'I' as well.

"Behind thy thoughts and feelings, my brother, standeth a mighty lord, an unknown wise man—whose name is self. In thy body he dwelleth, thy body he is.

"There is more reason in thy body than in thy best wisdom. And who can know why thy body needeth thy best wisdom?

"Thy self laugheth at thine 'I' and its prancings: What are these boundings and flights of thought? it saith unto itself. A round-about way to my purpose. I am the leading-string of the I and the suggester of its concepts.

"The creative self created for itself valuing and despising, it created for itself lust and woe. The creative body created for itself the spirit to be the hand of its will."

One of the best passages in Zarathustra's sermons is Nietzsche's command to love the overman, the man of the distant future:

"I tell you, your love of your neighbor is your bad love of yourselves.

"Ye flee from yourselves unto your neighbor and would fain make a virtue thereof; but I see through your 'unselfishness.'

"The thou is older than the I; the thou hath been proclaimed holy, but the I not yet; man thus thrusteth himself upon his neighbor.

"Do I counsel you to love your neighbor? I rather counsel you to flee from your neighbor and to love the most remote.

"Love unto the most remote future man is higher than love unto your neighbor. And I consider love unto things and ghosts to be higher than love unto men.

"This ghost which marcheth before thee, my brother, is more beautiful than thou art. Why dost thou not give him thy flesh and thy bones? Thou art afraid and fleest unto thy neighbor.

"Unable to endure yourselves and not loving yourselves enough, you seek to wheedle your neighbor into loving you and thus to gild you with his error.

"My brethren, I counsel you not to love your neighbor; I counsel you to love those who are the most remote."

In perfect agreement with the ideal of the overman is Nietzsche's view of marriage, and verily it contains a very true and noble thought:

"Thou shalt build beyond thyself. But first thou must be built thyself square in body and soul.

"Thou shalt not only propagate thyself but propagate thyself upwards! Therefore the garden of marriage may help thee!

"Thou shalt create a higher body, a prime motor, a wheel of self-rolling,—thou shalt create a creator.

"Marriage: thus I call the will of two to create that one which is more than they who created it. I call marriage reverence unto each other as unto those who will such a will.

"Let this be the significance and the truth of thy marriage. But that which the much-too-many call marriage, those superfluous—alas, what call I that?

"Alas! that soul's poverty of two! Alas! that soul's dirt of two! Alas! that miserable ease of two!

"Marriage they call that; and they say marriage is made in heaven.

"Well, I like it not, that heaven of the superfluous!"

Nietzsche takes a Schopenhauerian view of womankind, excepting from the common condemnation his sister alone, to whom he once said, "You are not a woman, you are a friend." He says of woman:

"Too long a slave and a tyrant have been hidden in woman. Therefore woman is not yet capable of friendship; she knoweth love only."

Nietzsche is not aware that the self changes and that it grows by the acquisition of truth. He treats the self as remaining the same, and truth as that which our will has made conceivable. Truth to him is a mere creature of the self. Here is Zarathustra's condemnation of man's search for truth:

"'Will unto truth' ye call, ye wisest men, what inspireth you and maketh you ardent?

"'Will unto the conceivableness of all that is,'—thus I call your will!

"All that is ye are going to *make* conceivable. For with good mistrust ye doubt whether it is conceivable.

"But it hath to submit itself and bend before yourselves! Thus your will willeth. Smooth it shall become and subject unto spirit as its mirror and reflected image.

"That is your entire will, ye wisest men, as a will unto power; even when ye speak of good and evil and of valuations.

"Ye will create the world before which to kneel down. Thus it is your last hope and drunkenness."

Recognition of truth is regarded as submission:

"To be true,—few are able to be so! And he who is able doth not want to be so. But least of all the good are able.

"Oh, these good people! *Good men never speak the truth.* To be good in that way is a sickness for the mind.

"They yield, these good men, they submit themselves; their heart saith what is said unto it, their foundation obeyeth. But whoever obeyeth doth not hear *himself!*"

Nietzsche despises science. He must have had sorry experiences with scientists who offered him the dry bones of scholarship as scientific truth.

"When I lay sleeping, a sheep ate at the ivy-wreath of my head,—ate and said eating: 'Zarathustra is no longer a scholar.'

"Said it and went off clumsily and proudly. So a child told me.

"This is the truth: I have departed from the house of scholars, and the door I have shut violently behind me.

"Too long sat my soul hungry at their table. Not, as they, am I trained for perceiving as for cracking nuts.

"Freedom I love, and a breeze over a fresh soil. And

I would rather sleep on ox-skins than on their honors and respectabilities.

"I am too hot and am burnt with mine own thoughts, so as often to take my breath away. Then I must go into the open air and away from all dusty rooms.

"Like millworks they work, and like corn-crushers. Let folk only throw their grain into them! They know only too well how to grind corn and make white dust out of it.

"They look well at each other's fingers and trust each other not over-much. Ingenious in little stratagems, they wait for those whose knowledge walketh on lame feet; like spiders they wait.

"They also know how to play with false dice; and I found them playing so eagerly that they perspired from it.

"We are strangers unto each other, and their virtues are still more contrary unto my taste than their falsehoods and false dice."

Even if all scientists were puny sciolists, the ideal of science would remain, and if all the professed seekers for truth were faithless to and unworthy of their high calling, truth itself would not be abolished.

So far as we can see, Nietzsche never became acquainted with any one of the exact sciences. He was a philologist who felt greatly dissatisfied with the loose methods of his colleagues, but he has not done much in his own specialty to attain to a greater exactness of results. His essays on Homer, on the Greek tragedy, and similar subjects, have apparently not received much recognition among philologists and historians.

Having gathered a number of followers in his cave, one of them, called the conscientious man, said to the others:

"We seek different things, even up here, ye and I. For I seek more security. Therefore have I come unto Zarathustra. For he is the firmest tower and will—

"Fear—that is man's hereditary and fundamental feeling. By fear everything is explained, original sin and original virtue. Out of fear also hath grown *my* virtue, which is called Science.

"Such long, old fears, at last become refined, spiritual, intellectual, to-day, methinketh, it is called *Science.*"

This conception of science is refuted by Nietzsche in this fashion:

"Thus spake the conscientious one. But Zarathustra, who had just returned into his cave and had heard the last speech and guessed its sense, threw a handful of roses at the conscientious one, laughing at his 'truths.' 'What?' he called. 'What did I hear just now? Verily, methinketh, thou art a fool, or I am one myself. And thy "truth" I turn upside down with one blow, and that quickly.'

"'For fear is our exception. But courage and adventure, and the joy of what is uncertain, what hath never been dared —courage, methinketh, is the whole prehistoric development of man.

"'From the wildest, most courageous beasts he hath, by his envy and his preying, won all their virtues. Only thus hath he become a man.

"'*This* courage, at last become refined, spiritual, intellectual, this human courage with an eagle's wings and a serpent's wisdom—it, methinketh, is called to-day—'

"'*Zarathustra!*' cried all who sat together there, as from one mouth making a great laughter withal."

In spite of identifying the self with the body, which is mortal, Nietzsche longs for the immortal. He says:

"Oh! how could I fail to be eager for eternity, and for the marriage-ring of rings, the ring of recurrence?

"Never yet have I found the woman by whom I should like to have had children, unless it be this woman I love—for I love thee, O Eternity!"

The best known of Nietzsche's poems forms the conclusion of *Thus Spake Zarathustra*, the most impress-

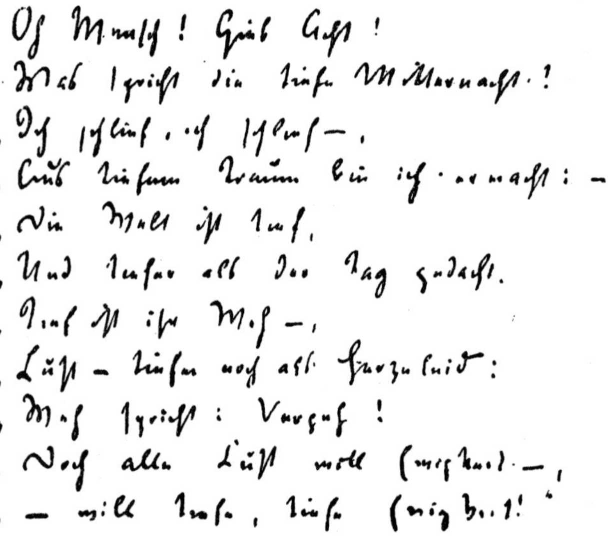

O Mensch! Gieb Acht!
„Was spricht die tiefe Mitternacht?
„Ich schlief, ich schlief —,
„Aus tiefem Traum bin ich erwacht: —
„Die Welt ist tief,
„Und tiefer als der Tag gedacht.
„Tief ist ihr Weh —,
„Lust — tiefer noch als Herzeleid:
„Weh spricht: Vergeh!
„Doch alle Lust will Ewigkeit —,
„— will tiefe, tiefe Ewigkeit!"

NIETZSCHE'S HANDWRITING.

ive work of Nietzsche, and is called by him "The Drunken Song." The thoughts are almost incoherent and it is difficult to say what is really meant by it. Nothing is more characteristic of Nietzsche's attitude and the vagueness of his fitful mode of thought. It

NIETZSCHE'S DRUNKEN SONG

ILLUSTRATION BY LINDLOF

has been illustrated by Hans Lindlof, in the same spirit in which Richard Strauss has written a musical composition on the theme of Nietzsche's *Thus Spake Zarathustra.*

"The Drunken Song" reads in our translation as follows:

"Man, listen, pray!
What the deep midnight has to say:
'I lay asleep,
'But woke from dreams deep and distraught.
'The world is deep,
'E'en deeper than the day e'er thought.
'Deep's the world's pain,—
'Joy deeper still than heartache's burning.
'Pain says, Life's vain!
'But for eternity Joy's yearning,
'For deep eternity Joy's yearning!'"

Prof. William Benjamin Smith has translated this same song, and we think it will be interesting to our readers to compare his translation with our rendering. It reads as follows:

"Oh Man! Give ear!
What saith the midnight deep and drear?
'From sleep, from sleep
'I woke as from a dream profound.
'The world is deep
'And deeper than the day can sound.
'Deep is its woe,—
'Joy, deeper still than heart's distress.
'Woe saith, Forego!
'But Joy wills everlastingness,—
'Wills deep, deep everlastingness.'"

A PROTEST AGAINST HIMSELF

NIETZSCHE is far from regarding his philosophy as timely. He was a proud and aristocratic character, spoiled from childhood by an unfaltering admiration on the part of both his mother and sister. It was unfortunate for him that his father had died before he could influence the early years of his son through wholesome discipline. Not enjoying a vigorous constitution Nietzsche was greatly impressed with the thought that a general decadence was overshadowing mankind. The truth was that his own bodily system was subject to many ailments which hampered his mental improvement. He was hungering for health, he envied the man of energy, he longed for strength and vigor, but all this was denied him, and so these very shortcomings of his own bodily strength—his own decadence—prompted in him a yearning for bodily health, for an unbounded exercise of energy, and for success. These were his dearest ideals, and his desire for power was his highest ambition. He saw in the history of human thought, the development of the notion of the "true world," which to him was a mere subjective phantom, a superstition; but a reaction would set in, and he prophesied that the doom of nihilism would sweep over the civilized world applying the torch to its temples, churches and institutions. Upon the ruins of the old world the real man, the overman, would rise and establish his own empire, an empire of unlimited power in which the herds, i. e., the common people would become subservient.

Nietzsche's philosophy forms a strange contrast to his own habits of life. A model of virtue, he made himself the advocate of vice, and gloried in it. He encouraged the robber[1] to rob, but he himself was honesty incarnate; he incited the people to rebel against authority of all kinds, but he himself was a "model child" in the nursery, a "model scholar" in school, and a "model soldier" while serving in the German army. His teachers as well as the officers of his regiment fail to find words enough *to praise Nietzsche's obedience.*[2]

Nietzsche's professors declare that he distinguished himself *"durch pünktlichen Gehorsam"* (p. 3); his sister tells us that she and her brother were *"ungeheuer artig, wahre Musterkinder"* (p. 36). He makes a good soldier, and, in spite of his denunciations of posing,

[1] *E. g.:* "Bitte nie! Lass dies Gewimmer!
Nimm, ich bitte dich, nimm immer!"

[2] Compare *Das Leben Friedrich Nietzsche's* by his sister, Elisabeth Förster-Nietzsche.

displays theatrical vanity in having himself photographed with drawn sword (the scabbard is missing). His martial mustache almost anticipates the tonsorial art of the imperial barber of the present Kaiser; and yet his spectacled eyes and good-natured features betray the peacefulness of his intentions. He plays the soldier only, and would have found difficulty in killing even a fly.

Nietzsche disclaims ever having learned anything in any school, but there never was a more grateful German pupil in Germany. He composed fervid poems on his school—the well known institution Schulpforta, which on account of its severe discipline he praises, not in irony but seriously, as the "narrow gate." [3]

Nietzsche denounces the German character, German institutions, and the German language, his mother-tongue, and is extremely unfair in his denunciations. He takes pleasure in the fact that *Deutsch* (see Ulfila's Bible translation) originally means "pagans or heathen," and hopes that the dear German people will earn the honor of being called pagans. *(La Gaya Scienza,* p. 176.) A reaction against his patriotism set in immediately after the war, when he became acquainted with the brutality of some vulgar specimens of the victorious nation,—most of them non-combatants.[4]

[3] *Leben,* pp. 90-97.

[4] (See, *e. g.,* Leben, II., 1, pp. 108-111.) "Nach dem Kriege missfiel mir der Luxus, die Franzosenverachtung," etc., p. 108.

FRIEDRICH NIETZSCHE

AS A VOLUNTEER IN THE GERMAN ARTILLERY, 1868

Nietzsche not only wrote in German and made the most involved constructions, but when the war broke out he asked his adopted country Switzerland, in which he had acquired citizenship after accepting a position as professor of classical languages at the University of Basel, for leave of absence to join the German army. In the Franco-Prussian war he might have had a chance to live up to his theories of struggle, but unfortunately the Swiss authorities did not allow him to join the army, and granted leave of absence only on condition that he would serve as a nurse. Such is the irony of fate. While Nietzsche stood up for a ruthless assertion of strength and for a suppression of sympathy which he denounced as a relic of the ethics

"Ich halte das jetzige Preussen für eine der Cultur höchst gefährliche Macht." Nietzsche ridicules the German language as barbarous in sound (*La Gaya Scienza,* pp. 138-140), "wälderhaft, heiser, wie aus räucherigen Stuben und unhöflichen Gegenden." Unique is the origin of the standard style of modern high German from the bureaucratic slang, "kanzleimässig schreiben, das war etwas Vornehmes" (*La Gaya Scienza,* p. 138), and at present the German changes into an "Offizierdeutsch" (*ibid.,* p. 139). Nietzsche suspects "the German depth," "die deutsche Tiefe," to be a mere mental dyspepsia (see "Jenseits von Gut und Böse," p. 211), saying, "Der Deutsche verdaut seine Ereignisse schlecht, or wird nie damit fertig; die deutsche Tiefe ist oft nur eine schwere, zögernde Verdauung." Nevertheless, he holds that the old-fashioned German depth is better than modern Prussian "Sch..eidigkeit und Berliner Witz und Sand." He prefers the company of the Swiss to that of his countrymen. (See also "Was den Deutschen abgeht," Vol. 8, p. 108.)

of a negation of life, his own tender soul was so oversensitive that his sister feels justified in tracing his disease back to the terrible impressions he received during the war.

Nietzsche speaks of the king as "the dear father of the country."[5] If there was a flaw in Nietzsche's moral character, it was goody-goodyness; and his philosophy is a protest against the principles of his own nature. While boldly calling himself "the first unmoralist," justifying even license itself and defending the coarsest lust,[6] his own life might have earned him the name of sissy, and he shrank in disgust from moral filth wherever he met with it in practical life.

Nietzsche denounced pessimism, and yet his philosophy was, as he himself confesses, the last consequence of pessimism. Hegel declared (says Nietzsche in *Morgenröthe,* p. 8), "Contradiction moves the world, all things are self-contradictory"; "we (adds Nietzsche) carry pessimism even into logic." He proposes to vivisect morality; "but (adds he) you cannot vivisect a thing without killing it." Thus his "unmoralism" is simply an expression of his earnestness to in-

[5] "Unser lieber König," "der Landesvater," etc. See *Leben,* I., p. 24, and II., 1, p. 248, "Unser lieber alter Kaiser Wilhelm," and "wir Preussen waren wirklich stolz." These expressions occur in Nietzsche's description of the Emperor's appearance at Bayreuth.

[6] *E. g.,* "Auch der schädlichste Mensch ist vielleicht immer noch der allernützlichste in Hinsicht auf Erhaltung der Art," etc. *La Gaya Scienza,* p. 3 ff.

vestigate the moral problem, and he expresses the result in the terse sentence; *Moral ist Nothlüge (Menschliches,* p. 63.)

He preached struggle and hatred, and yet was so tender-hearted that in an hour of dejection he confessed to his sister with a sigh: "I was not at all made to hate or be an enemy."[7] The decadence which he imputes to mankind is a mere reflection of his own state of mind, and the strength which he praises is that quality in which he is most sorely lacking. Nietzsche himself had the least possible connection with active life. He was unmarried, had no children, nor any interests beyond his ambition, and having served as professor of the classical languages for some time at the small university of Basel, he was for the greater part of his life without a calling, without duties, without aims. He never ventured to put his own theories into practice. He did not even try to rise as a prophet of his own philosophy, and remained in isolation to the very end of his life.

Nietzsche must have felt the contradiction between his theories and his habits of life, and it appears that he suffered under it more than can be estimated by an impartial reader of his books. He was like the bird in the cage who sings of liberty, or an apoplectic patient who dreams of deeds of valor as a knight in tournament or as a wrestler in the prize ring. Never

[7] "Ich bin so gar nicht zum Hassen und zum Feind sein gemacht!"

was craving for power more closely united with impotence!

It is characteristic of him that he said, "If there were a God, how should I endure not to be God?" and so his ambition impelled him at least to prophesy the coming of his ideal, i. e., robust health, full of bodily vigor and animal spirits, unchecked by any rule of morality, and an unstinted use of power.

Nietzsche had an exaggerated conception of his vocation and he saw in himself the mouthpiece of that grandest and deepest truth, viz., that man should dare to be himself without any regard of morality or consideration for his fellow beings. And here we have the tragic element of his life. Nietzsche, the atheist, deemed himself a God incarnate, and the despiser of the Crucified, suffered a martyr's fate in offering his own life to the cause of his hope. The earnestness with which he preached his wild and untenable doctrines appeals to us and renders his figure sympathetic, which otherwise would be grotesque. Think of a man who in his megalomania preaches a doctrine that justifies an irresponsible desire for power! Would he not be ridiculous in his impotence to actualize his dream? and on the other hand, if he were strong enough to practice what he preached, if like another Napoleon, he would make true his dreams of enslaving the world, would not mankind in self-defense soon rise in rebellion and treat him as a criminal, rendering him and his followers incapable of doing harm? But Nietzsche's personality, weak and impotent and powerless to appear as the overman and to subjugate the world to his will, suffered excruciating pains in his soul and tormented himself to death, which came to him in the form of decadence—a softening of the brain.

Poor Nietzsche! what a bundle of contradictions! None of these contradictions are inexplicable. All of them are quite natural. They are the inevitable reactions against a prior enthusiasm, and he swings, according to the law of the pendulum, to the opposite extreme of his former position.

How did Nietzsche develop into an unmoralist? Simply by way of reaction against the influence of Schopenhauer in combination with the traditional Christianity.

Nietzsche passed through three periods in his development. He was first a follower of Schopenhauer and an admirer of Wagner, but he shattered his idols and became a convert to Auguste Comte's positivism. Schopenhauer was the master at whose feet Nietzsche sat; from him he learned boldness of thought and atheism, that this world is a world of misery and struggle. He accepted for a time Schopenhauer's pessimism but rebelled in his inmost soul against the ethical doctrine of the negation of the will. He retained Schopenhauer's contempt for previous philosophers (presumably he never tried to understand them) yet he resented the thought of a negation of life and replaced it by a most emphatic assertion. He thus recognized the reactionary spirit of

FRIEDRICH NIETZSCHE

AS PROFESSOR AT BASLE

Schopenhauer, whose system is a Christian metaphysics. Nietzsche denounces the ethics of a negation of the will as a disease, and since nature in the old system is regarded as the source of moral evil the idea dawns on him that he himself, trying to establish a philosophy of nature, is an immoralist. He now questions morality itself from the standpoint of an affirmation of the will, and at last goes so far as to speak of ideals as a symptom of shallowness.[8]

Nietzsche argued that our conception of truth and our ideal world is but a phantasmagoria, and the picture of the universe in our consciousness a distorted image of real life. Our pleasures and pains, too, are both transient and subjective. Accordingly it would be a gross mistake for us to exaggerate their importance. What does it matter if we endure a little more or less pain, or of what use are the pleasures in which we might indulge? The realities of life consist in power, and in our dominion over the forces that dominate life. Knowledge and truth are of no use unless they become subservient to this realistic desire for power. They are mere means to an end which is the superiority of the overman, the representative of Nietzsche's philosophy by whom the mass of mankind are to be enslaved. This view constitutes his third

[8] See, e. g., *Leben,* I., p. 135, where he speaks of a new "Freigeisterei," denouncing the "libres penseurs" as "unverbesserliche Flachköpfe und Hanswürste," adding, "Sie glauben allesammt noch an's 'Ideal.'"

period, in which he wrote those works that are peculiarly characteristic of his own philosophy.

Nietzsche must not be taken too seriously. He was engaged with the deepest problems of life, and published his opinions as to their solution before he had actually attempted to investigate them. He criticised and attacked like the Irishman who hits a head wherever he sees it. Here are the first three rules of his philosophical warfare:

"First: I attack only those causes which are victorious, sometimes I wait till they are victorious. Secondly: I attack them only when I would find no allies, when I stand isolated, when I compromise myself alone. Thirdly: I have never taken a step in public which did not compromise me. That is my criterion of right action."

A man who adopts this strange criterion of right conduct must produce a strange philosophy. His soul is in an uproar against itself. Says Nietzsche in his *Götzendämmerung*, Aphorism 45:

> "Almost every genius knows as one phase of his development the 'Catilinary existence,' so-called, which is a feeling of hatred, of vengeance, of revolution against everything that is, which no longer needs to become . . . Catiline—the form of Cæsar's pre-existence."

Nietzsche changed his views during his life-time, and the unmoralist Nietzsche originated in contradiction to his habitual moralism. He was a man of extremes. As soon as a new thought dawned on him, it took possession of his soul to the exclusion of his prior views, and his later self contradicts his former self.

Nietzsche says:

"The serpent that cannot slough must die. In the same way, the spirits which are prevented from changing their opinions cease to be spirits."

So we must expect that if Nietzsche had been permitted to continue longer in health, he would have cast off the slough of his immoralism and the negative conceptions of his positivism. His *Zarathustra* was the last work of his pen, but it is only the most classical expression of the fermentation of his soul, not the final purified result of his philosophy; it is not the solution of the problem that stirred his heart.

While writing his *Unzeitgemässe Betrachtungen*, Nietzsche characterizes his method of work thus:

"That I proceed with my outpourings considerably like a dilettante and in an immature manner, I know very well, but I am anxious first of all to get rid of the whole polemico-negative material. I wish undisturbedly to sing off, up and down and truly dastardly, the whole gamut of my hostile feelings, 'that the vaults shall echo back.'[*] Later on, i. e., within five years, I shall discard all polemics and bethink myself of a really 'good work.' But at present my breast is oppressed with disgust and tribulation. I must expectorate, decorously and indecorously, but radically and for good" [*endgültig*].

The writings of Nietzsche will make the impression of a youthful immaturity upon any half-way serious

[*] "Dass das Gewölbe wiederhallt,"—a quotation from Goethe's "Faust."

reader. There is a hankering after originality which of necessity leads to aberrations and a sovereign contempt for the merits of the past. The world seems endangered, and yet any one who would seriously try to live up to Nietzsche's ideal must naturally sober down after a while, and we may apply to him what Mephistopheles says of the baccalaureus:

> "Yet even from him we're not in special peril
> He will, ere long, to other thoughts incline.
> The must may foam absurdly in the barrel,
> Nathless, it turns at last to wine."
>
> *Tr. by Bayard Taylor.*

Nietzsche did not live long enough to experience a period of matured thought. He died before the fermentation of his mind had come to its normal close, and so his life will remain forever a great torso, without intrinsic worth, but suggestive and appealing only to the immature, including the "herd animal" who would like to be an overman.

The very immaturity of Nietzsche's view becomes attractive to immature minds. He wrote while his thoughts were still in a state of fermentation, and he died before the wine of his soul was clarified.

Nietzsche is an almost tragic figure that will live in art as a brooding thinker, a representative of the dissatisfied, a man of an insatiable love of life, with wild and unsteady looks, proud in his indomitable self-assertion, but broken in body and spirit. Such he was in his last disease when his mind was wrapt in the eternal night of dementia, the oppressive conscious-

FRIEDRICH NIETZSCHE

THE LATEST PORTRAIT, AFTER AN OIL PAINTING
BY C. STOEVING

ness of which made him exclaim in lucid moments the pitiable complaint, *"Mutter, ich bin dumm."* As such he is represented in Klein's statue,[10] which in its pathetic posture is a psychological masterpiece.

Nietzsche's works are poetic effusions more than philosophical expositions and yet we would hesitate to call him a poet. His poems are not poetical in the usual sense. They lack poetry and yet they appeal not only to his admirers, but also to his critics and enemies. Most of them are artificial yet they are so characteristic that they are interesting specimens of a peculiar kind of taste. They strike us as ingenious, because they reflect his eccentricities.

In a poem entitled "Ecce Homo"[11] he characterizes himself:

> "Yea, I know from whence I came!
> Never satiate, like the flame
> Glow I and consume me too
> Into light turns what I find,
> Cinders do I leave behind,
> Flame am I, 'tis surely true."

[11] "Ja, ich weiss woher ich stamme!
Ungesättigt gleich der Flamme,
Glühe und verzehr ich mich,
Licht wird alles was ich fasse,
Kohle alles was ich lasse:
Flamme bin ich sicherlich!"

[10] Reproduced as the frontispiece of this book.

NIETZSCHE'S PREDECESSOR

FRIEDRICH NIETZSCHE, the author of *Thus Spake Zarathustra* and the inventor of the new ideal called the "overman," is commonly regarded as the most extreme egotist, to whom morality is non-existent and who glories in the coming of the day in which a man of his liking—the overman—would live *au grand jour.* His philosophy is an individualism carried to its utmost extreme, sanctioning egotism, denouncing altruism and establishing the right of the strong to trample the weak under foot. It is little known, however, that he followed another thinker, Johann Caspar Schmidt, whose extreme individualism he adopted. But this forerunner who preached a philosophy of the sovereignty of self and an utter disregard of our neighbors' rights remained unheeded; he lived in obscurity, he died in poverty, and under the pseudonym "Max Stirner" he left behind a book entitled *Der Einzige und sein Eigentum.*

The historian Lange briefly mentioned him in his *History of Materialism,* and the novelist John Henry

Mackay followed up the reference which led to the discovery of this lonely comet on the philosophical sky.[1]

The strangest thing about this remarkable book consists in the many coincidences with Friedrich Nietzsche's philosophy. It is commonly deemed impossible that the famous spokesman of the overman should not have been thoroughly familiar with this failure in the philosophical book market; but while Stirner was forgotten the same ideas transplanted into the volumes of the author of *Thus Spake Zarathustra* found an echo first in Germany and soon afterwards all over the world.

Stirner's book has been Englished by Stephen T. Byington with an introduction by J. L. Walker at the instigation of Benjamin R. Tucker, the representative of American peaceful anarchism, under the title *The Ego and His Own.* They have been helped by Mr. George Schumm and his wife, Mrs. Emma Heller Schumm. These five persons, all interested in this lonely and unique thinker, must have had much trouble in translating the German original and though the final rendering of the title is not inappropriate, the translator and his advisers agree that it falls short of the mark. For the accepted form Mr. B. R. Tucker is responsible, and he admits in the preface that it is not

[1] See also R. Schellwien, *Max Stirner und Friedrich Nietzsche;* V. Basch, *L'individualisme anarchiste, Max Stirner,* 1904.

an exact equivalent of the German. *Der Einzige* means "the unique man," a person of a definite individuality, but in the book itself our author modifies and enriches the meaning of the term. The unique man becomes the ego and an owner (*ein Eigener*), a man who is possessed of property, especially of his own being. He is a master of his own and he prides himself on his ownhood, as well as his ownership. As such he is unique, and the very term indicates that the thinker who proposes this view-point is an extreme individualist. In Stirner's opinion Christianity pursued the ideal of liberty from the world; and in this sense Christians speak of spiritual liberty. To become free from anything that oppresses us we must get rid of it, and so the Christian to rid himself of the world becomes a prey to the idea of a contempt of the world. Stirner declares that the future has a better lot in store for man. Man shall not merely be free, which is a purely negative quality, but he shall be his own master; he shall become an owner of his own personality and whatever else he may have to control. His end and aim is he himself. There is no moral duty above him. Stirner explains in the very first sentence of his book:

> "What is not supposed to be my concern! First and foremost, the good cause, then God's cause, the cause of mankind, of truth, of freedom, of humanity, of justice; further, the cause of my people, my prince, my fatherland; finally, even the cause of mind, and a thousand other causes. Only *my* cause is never to be my concern. 'Shame on the egoist who thinks only of himself.'"

Stirner undertakes to refute this satirical explanation in his book on the unique man and his own, and a French critic according to Paul Lauterbach (p. 5) speaks of his book as *un livre qu'on quitte monarque,* "a book which one lays aside a king."

Stirner is opposed to all traditional views. He is against church and state. He stands for the self-development of every individual, and insists that the highest duty of every one is to stand up for his ownhood.

J. L. Walker in his Introduction contrasts Stirner with Nietzsche and gives the prize of superiority to the former, declaring him to be a genuine anarchist not less than Josiah Warren, the leader of the small band of New England anarchists. He says:

"In Stirner we have the philosophical foundation for political liberty. His interest in the practical development of egoism to the dissolution of the state and the union of free men is clear and pronounced, and harmonizes perfectly with the economic philosophy of Josiah Warren. Allowing for difference of temperament and language, there is a substantial agreement between Stirner and Proudhon. Each would be free, and sees in every increase of the number of free people and their intelligence an auxiliary force against the oppressor. But, on the other hand, will any one for a moment seriously contend that Nietzsche and Proudhon march together in general aim and tendency—that they have anything in common except the daring to profane the shrine and sepulcher of superstition?

"Nietzsche has been much spoken of as a disciple of Stirner, and, owing to favorable cullings from Nietzsche's writings, it has occurred that one of his books has been supposed to contain more sense than it really does—so long as one had read only the extracts.

"Nietzsche cites scores or hundreds of authors. Had he read everything, and not read Stirner?

"But Nietzsche is as unlike Stirner as a tight-rope performance is unlike an algebraic equation.

"Stirner loved liberty for himself, and loved to see any and all men and women taking liberty, and he had no lust of power. Democracy to him was sham liberty, egoism the genuine liberty.

"Nietzsche, on the contrary, pours out his contempt upon democracy because it is not aristocratic. He is predatory to the point of demanding that those who must succumb to feline rapacity shall be taught to submit with resignation. When he speaks of 'anarchistic dogs' scouring the streets of great civilized cities, it is true, the context shows that he means the communists; but his worship of Napoleon, his bathos of anxiety for the rise of an aristocracy that shall rule Europe for thousands of years, his idea of treating women in the Oriental fashion, show that Nietzsche has struck out in a very old path—doing the apotheosis of tyranny. We individual egoistic anarchists, however, may say to the Nietzsche school, so as not to be misunderstood: We do not ask of the Napoleons to have pity, nor of the predatory barons to do justice. They will find it convenient for their own welfare to make terms with men who have learned of Stirner what a man can be who worships nothing, bears allegiance to nothing. To Nietzsche's rhodomontade of eagles in baronial form, born to prey on industrial lambs, we rather tauntingly oppose the ironical question: Where are your claws? What if the 'eagles' are found to be plain barnyard fowls on which more silly fowls have fastened steel spurs to hack the victims, who, however, have the power to disarm the sham 'eagles' between two suns?

"Stirner shows that men make their tyrants as they make their gods, and his purpose is to unmake tyrants.

"Nietzsche dearly loves a tyrant.

"In style Stirner's work offers the greatest possible contrast to the puerile, padded phraseology of Nietzsche's *Zarathustra* and its false imagery. Who ever imagined such an unnatural conjuncture as an eagle 'toting' a serpent in friendship? which performance is told of in bare words, but nothing comes of it. In Stirner we are treated to an enlivening and earnest discussion addressed to serious minds, and every reader feels that the word is to him, for his instruction and benefit, so far as he has mental independence and courage to take it and use it. The startling intrepidity of this book is infused with a whole-hearted love for all mankind, as evidenced by the fact that the author shows not one iota of prejudice or any idea of division of men into ranks. He would lay aside government, but would establish any regulation deemed convenient, and for this only *our* convenience is consulted. Thus there will be general liberty only when the disposition toward tyranny is met by intelligent opposition that will no longer submit to such a rule. Beyond this the manly sympathy and philosophical bent of Stirner are such that rulership appears by contrast a vanity, an infatuation of perverted pride. We know not whether we more admire our author or more love him.

"Stirner's attitude toward woman is not special. She is an individual if she can be, not handicapped by anything he says, feels, thinks, or plans. This was more fully exemplified in his life than even in this book; but there is not a line in the book to put or keep woman in an inferior position to man, neither is there anything of caste or aristocracy in the book."

It is not our intention to enter here into a detailed criticism of Stirner's book. We will only point out that society will practically remain the same whether we consider social arrangements as voluntary contracts or as organically developed social institutions, or as imposed upon mankind by the divine world-order, or even if czars and kings claim to govern "by the grace of God." Whatever religious or natural sanction any government may claim to possess, the method of keeping order will be the same everywhere. Wrongs have been done and in the future may still be committed in the name of right, and injustice may again and again worst justice in the name of the law. On the other hand, however, we can notice a progress throughout the world of a slow but steady improvement of conditions. Any globe-trotter will find by experience that his personal safety, his rights and privileges are practically the same in all civilized countries, whether they are republics like Switzerland, France and the United States, or monarchies like Sweden, Germany and Italy. At the same time murders, robberies, thefts and other crimes are committed all over the world, even in the homes of those who pride themselves on being the most civilized nations. The world-conception lying behind our different social theories is the same wherever the same kind of civilization prevails. Where social evils prevail, dissatisfaction sets in which produces theories and reform programs, and when they remain unheeded, a climax is reached which leads to revolution.

Stirner's book begins with a short exhortation headed with Goethe's line,

> "My trust in nothingness is placed."

He discusses the character of human life (Chap. I) and contrasts men of the old and the new eras (Chap. II). He finds that the ancients idealized bodily existence while Christianity incarnates the ideal. Greek artists transfigure actual life; in Christianity the divine takes abode in the world of flesh, God becomes incarnate in man. The Greeks tried to go beyond the world and Christianity came; Christian thinkers are pressed to go beyond God, and there they find spirit. They are led to a contempt of the world and will finally end in a contempt of spirit. But Stirner believes that the ideal and the real can never be reconciled, and we must free ourselves from the errors of the past. The truly free man is not the one who has become free, but the one who has come into his own, and this is the sovereign ego.

As Achilles had his Homer so Stirner found his prophet in a German socialist of Scotch Highlander descent, John Henry Mackay. The reading public should know that Mackay belongs to the same type of restless reformers, and he soon became an egoistic anarchist, a disciple of Stirner. His admiration is but a natural consequence of conditions. Nevertheless Mackay's glorification of Stirner proves that in Stirner this onesided world-conception has found its classical, its most consistent and its philosophically most systematic presentation. Whatever we may have to criticize in anarchism, Stirner is a man of uncommon distinction, the leader of a party, and the standard-bearer of a cause distinguished by the extremeness of its propositions which from the principle of individualism are carried to their consistent ends.

Mackay undertook the difficult task of unearthing the history of a man who, naturally modest and retired, had nowhere left deep impressions. No stone remained unturned and every clue that could reveal anything about his hero's life was followed up with unprecedented devotion. He published the results of his labors in a book entitled "Max Stirner, His Life and His Work."[2] The report is extremely touching not so much on account of the great significance of Stirner's work which to impartial readers appears exaggerated, but through the personal tragedy of a man who towers high above his surroundings and suffers the misery of poverty and failure.

Mr. Mackay describes Stirner as of medium height, rather less so than more, well proportioned, slender, always dressed with care though without pretension, having the appearance of a teacher, and wearing silver- or steel-rimmed spectacles. His hair and beard were blonde with a tinge of red, his eyes blue and clear, but neither dreamy nor penetrating. His thin lips usually wore a sarcastic smile, which, however, had nothing of bitterness; his general appearance was sympathetic. No portrait of Stirner is in existence except one pencil sketch which was made from memory in

[2]*Max Stirner, sein Leben und sein Werk.* Berlin, 1898.

1892 by the London socialist, Friedrich Engels, but the criticism is made by those who knew Stirner that his features, especially his chin and the top of his head, were not so angular though nose and mouth are said

Pencil Sketch of Max Stirner.
The only portrait in existence.

to have been well portrayed, and Mackay claims that Stirner never wore a coat and collar of that type.

Stirner was of purely Frankish blood. His ancestors lived for centuries in or near Baireuth. His father, Albert Christian Heinrich Schmidt of Anspach, a maker of wind-instruments, died of consumption in 1807 at the age of 37, half a year after the birth of his son. His mother, Sophie Eleanora, née Reinlein of the city of Erlangen, six months later married H. F.

L. Ballerstedt, the assistant in an apothecary shop in Helmstedt, and moved with him to Kulm on the Vistula. In 1818 the boy was sent back to his native city where his childless god-father and uncle, Johann Caspar Martin Sticht, and his wife took care of him.

Young Johann Caspar passed through school with credit, and his schoolmates used to call him "Stirner" on account of his high forehead (*Stirn*) which was the most conspicuous feature of his face. This name clung to him throughout life. In fact his most intimate friends never called him by any other, his real name being almost forgotten through disuse and figuring only in official documents.

Stirner attended the universities of Erlangen, Berlin and Königsberg, and finally passed his examination for admission as a teacher in gymnasial schools. His stepfather died in the summer of 1837 in Kulm at the age of 76. It is not known what became of his mother who had been mentally unsound for some time.

Neither father nor stepfather had ever been successful, and if Stirner ever received any inheritance it must have been very small. On December 12 of 1837 Stirner married Agnes Clara Kunigunde Burtz, the daughter of his landlady.

Their married life was brief, the young wife dying in a premature child-birth on August 29th. We have no indication of an ardent love on either side. He who wrote with passionate fire and with so much insistence in his philosophy, was calm and peaceful, subdued and quiet to a fault in real life.

Having been refused appointment in one of the public or royal schools Stirner accepted a position in a girls' school October 1, 1839. During the political fermentation which preceded the revolutionary year of 1848, he moved in the circle of those bold spirits who called themselves *Die Freien* and met at Hippel's, among whom were Ludwig Buhl, Meyen, Friedrich Engels, Mussak, C. F. Köppen, the author of a work on Buddha, Dr. Arthur Müller and the brothers Bruno, Egbert and Edgar Bauer. It was probably among their associates that Stirner met Marie Dähnhardt of Gadebusch near Schwerin, Mecklenberg, the daughter of an apothecary, Helmuth Ludwig Dähnhardt. She was as different from Stirner as a dashing emancipated woman can be from a gentle meek man, but these contrasts were joined together in wedlock on October 21, 1843. Their happiness did not last long, for Marie Dähnhardt left her husband at the end of three years.

The marriage ceremony of this strange couple has been described in the newspapers and it is almost the only fact of Stirner's life that stands out boldly as a well-known incident. That these descriptions contain exaggerations and distortions is not improbable, but it cannot be denied that much contained in the reports must be true.

On the morning of October 21, a clergyman of extremely liberal views, Rev. Marot, a member of the Consistory, was called to meet the witnesses of the ceremony at Stirner's room. Bruno Bauer, Buhl, probably also Julius Faucher, Assessor Kochius and a young English woman, a friend of the bride, were present. The bride was in her week-day dress. Mr. Marot asked for a Bible, but none could be found. According to one version the clergyman was obliged to request Herr Buhl to put on his coat and to have the cards removed. When the rings were to be exchanged the groom discovered that he had forgotten to procure them, and according to Wilhelm Jordan's recollection Bauer pulled out his knitted purse and took off the brass rings, offering them as a substitute during the ceremony. After the wedding a dinner with cold punch was served to which Mr. Marot was invited. But he refused, while the guests remained and the wedding carousal proceeded in its jolly course.

In order to understand how this incident was possible we must know that in those pre-revolutionary years the times were out of joint and these heroes of the rebellion wished to show their disrespect and absolute indifference to a ceremony that to them had lost all its sanctity.

Stirner's married life was very uneventful, except that he wrote the main book of his life and dedicated it to his wife after a year's marriage, with the words,

"Meinem Liebchen
Marie Dähnhardt."

Obviously this form which ignores the fact that they were married, and uses a word of endearment which in this connection is rather trivial, must be regarded as characteristic of their relation and their life principles. Certain it is that she understood only the negative features of her husband's ideals and had no appreciation of the genius that stirred within him. Lauterbach, the editor of the Reclam edition of Stirner's book, comments ironically on this dedication with the Spanish motto *Da Dios almendras al que no tiene muelas,* "God gives almonds to those who have no teeth."

Marie Dähnhardt was a graceful blonde woman rather under-sized, with heavy hair which surrounded her head in ringlets according to the fashion of the time. She was very striking and became a favorite of the round table of the *Freien* who met at Hippel's. She smoked cigars freely and sometimes donned male attire, in order to accompany her husband and his friends on their nightly excursions. It appears that Stirner played the most passive part in these adventures, but true to his principle of individuality we have no knowledge that he ever criticized his wife.

Marie Dähnhardt had lost her father early and was in possession of a small fortune of 10,000 thalers, possibly more. At any rate it was considered quite a sum in the circle of Stirner's friends, but it did not last long. Having written his book, Stirner gave up his position so as to prevent probable discharge and now they looked around for new resources. Though Stirner had studied political economy he was a most unpractical man; but seeing there was a dearth of milk-shops, he and his wife started into business. They made contracts with dairies but did not advertise their shop, and when the milk was delivered to them they had large quantities of milk on hand but no patrons, the result being a lamentable failure with debts.

In the circle of his friends Stirner's business experience offered inexhaustible material for jokes, while at home it led rapidly to the dissolution of his marriage. Frau Schmidt complained in later years that her husband had wasted her property, while no complaints are known from him. One thing is sure that they separated. She went to England where she established herself as a teacher under the protection of Lady Bunsen, the wife of the Prussian ambassador.

Frau Schmidt's later career is quite checkered. She was a well-known character in the colony of German exiles in London. One of her friends there was a Lieutenant Techow. When she was again in great distress she emigrated with other Germans, probably in 1852 or 1853, to Melbourne, Australia. Here she tasted the misery of life to the dregs. She made a living as a washerwoman and is reported to have married a day laborer. Their bitter experiences made her resort to religion for consolation, and in 1870 or 1871 she became a convert to the Catholic Church. At her sister's death she became her heir and so restored her good fortune to some extent. She returned to London where Mr. Mackay to his great joy discovered that she was still alive at the advanced age of eighty. What a valuable resource her reminiscences would be for his inquiries! But she refused to give any information and finally wrote him a letter which literally reads as follows: "Mary Smith *solemnly avowes* that she will have *no more* correspondence on the subject, and authorizes Mr. ———[3] to return all those writings to their owners. She is ill and prepares for death."

The last period of Stirner's life, from the time when his wife left him to his death, is as obscure as his childhood days. He moved from place to place, and since his income was very irregular creditors pressed him hard. His lot was tolerable because of the simple habits of his life, his only luxury consisting in smoking a good cigar. In 1853 we find him at least twice in debtor's prison, first 21 days, from March 5 to 26, 1853, and then 36 days, from New Year's eve until February 4 of the next year. In the meantime (September 7) he moved to Philippstrasse 19. It was Stirner's last home. He stayed with the landlady of this place, a kind-hearted woman who treated all her boarders like a mother, until June 25, 1856, when he died rather suddenly as the result of the bite of a poisonous fly. A few of his friends, among them Bruno Bauer and Ludwig Buhl, attended his funeral; a second-class

[3] The name of the gentleman she mentions is replaced by a dash at his express wish in the facsimile of her letter reproduced in Mr. Mackay's book (p. 255).

grave was procured for one thaler 10 groats, amounting approximately to one American dollar.

During this period Stirner undertook several literary labors from which he possibly procured some remuneration. He translated the classical authors on political economy from the French and from the English, which appeared under the title *Die National-Oekonomen der Franzosen und Engländer* (Leipsic, Otto Wigand, 1845-1847).

He also wrote a history of the Reaction which he explained to be a mere counter-revolution. This *Geschichte der Reaction* was planned as a much more comprehensive work, but the two volumes which appeared were only two parts of the second volume as originally intended.

The work is full of quotations, partly from Auguste Comte, partly from Edmund Burke. None of these works represent anything typically original or of real significance in the history of human thought.

His real contribution to the world's literature remains his work *Der Einzige und sein Eigentum,* the title of which is rendered in English *The Ego and His Own,* and this, strange to say, enthrones the individual man, the ego, every personality, as a sovereign power that should not be subject to morality, rules, obligations, or duties of any kind. The appeal is made so directly that it will convince all those unscientific and half-educated minds who after having surrendered their traditional faith find themselves without any authority in either religion or politics. God is to them a fable and the state an abstraction. Ideas and ideals, such as truth, goodness, beauty, are mere phrases. What then remains but the concrete bodily personality of every man of which every one is the ultimate standard of right and wrong?

EGO-SOVEREIGNTY

STRANGE that neither of these philosophers of individuality, Nietzsche or Stirner, ever took the trouble to investigate what an individual is! Stirner halts before this most momentous question of his world-conception, and so he overlooks that his ego, his own individuality, this supreme sovereign standing beyond right and wrong, the ultimate authority of everything, is a hazy, fluctuating, uncertain thing which differs from day to day and finally disappears.

The individuality of any man is the product of communal life. No one of us could exist as a rational personality were he not a member of a social group from which he has imbibed his ideas as well as his language. Every word is a product of his intercourse with his fellow-beings. His entire existence consists in his relations toward others and finds expression in his attitude toward social institutions. We may criticize existent institutions but we can never do without any. A denial of either their existence or their significance proves an utter lack of insight into the nature of personality.

We insert here a few characteristic sentences of Stirner's views, and in order to be fair we follow the condensation of John Henry Mackay (pp. 135-192) than whom certainly we could find no more sympathetic or intelligent student of this individualistic philosophy.

Here are Stirner's arguments:

The ancients arrived at the conclusion that man was spirit. They created a world of spirit, and in this world of spirit Christianity begins. But what is spirit? Spirit has originated from nothing. It is its own creation and man makes it the center of the world. The injunction was given, Thou shalt not live to thyself but to thy spirit, to thy ideas. Spirit is the God, the ego and the spirit are in constant conflict. Spirit dwells beyond the earth. It is in vain to force the divine into service here for I am neither God nor man, neither the highest being nor my being. The spirit is like a ghost whom no one has seen, but of whom there are innumerable creditable witnesses, such as grandmother can give account of. The whole world that surrounds thee is filled with spooks of thy imagination. The holiness of truth which hallows thee is a strange element. It is not thine own and strangeness is a characteristic of holiness. The specter is truly only in thine ownhood . . . . . Right is a spleen conferred by a spook; might, that is myself. I am the mighty one and the owner of might . . . . . Right is the royal will of society. Every right which exists is created right. I am expected to honor it where I find it and subject myself to it. But what to me is the right of society, the right of all? What do I care for equality of right, for the struggle for right, for inalienable rights? Right becomes word in law. The dominant will is the preserver of the states. My own will shall upset them. Every state is a despotism. All right and all power is claimed to belong to the community of the people. I, however, shall not allow myself to be bound by it, for I recognize no duty even though the state may call crime in me what it considers right for itself. My relation to the state is not the relation of one ego to another ego. It is the relation of the sinner to the saint, but the saint is a mere fixed idea from which crimes originate (Mackay, pages 154-5).

It will sometimes be difficult to translate Stirner's declarations in their true meaning; for instance: "I am the owner of mankind, I am mankind and shall do nothing for the benefit of another mankind. The property of mankind is mine. I do not respect the property of mankind. Poverty originates when I can not utilize my own self as I want to. It is the state which hinders men from entering into a direct relation with others. On the mercy of right my private property depends. Only within prescribed limits am I allowed to compete. Only the medium of exchange, the money which the state makes, am I allowed to use. The forms of the state may change, the purpose of the state always remains the same. My property, however, is what I empower myself to. Let violence decide, I expect all from my own.

"You shall not lure me with love, nor catch me with the promise of communion of possessions, but the question of property will be solved only through a war of all against all, and what a slave will do as soon as he has broken his fetters we shall have to see. I know no law of love. As every one of my sentiments is my property, so also is love. I give it, I donate it, I squander it merely because it makes me happy. Earn it if you believe you have a right to it. The measure of my sentiments can not be prescribed to me, nor the aim of my feelings determined. We and the world have only one relation toward each other, that of usefulness. Yea, I use the world and men." (Pp. 156-157.)

As to promises made and confidence solicited Stirner would not allow a limitation of freedom. He says: "In itself an oath is no more sacred than a lie is contemptible." Stirner opposes the idea of communism. "The community of man creates laws for society. Communism is a communion in equality." Says Stirner, "I prefer to depend on the egotism of men rather than on their compassion." He feels himself swelled into a temporary, transient, puny deity. No man expresses him rightly, no concept defines him; he, the ego, is perfect. Stirner concludes his book: "Owner I am of my own power and I am such only when I know myself as the only one. In the only one even the owner returns into his creative nothingness from which he was born. Any higher being above, be it God or man, detracts from the feeling of my uniqueness and it pales before the sun of this consciousness. If I place my trust in myself, the only one, it will stand upon a transient mortal creator of himself, who feeds upon himself, and I can say,

"Ich hab mein Sach' auf nichts gestellt."
"My trust in nothingness is placed."

We call attention to Stirner's book, "The Only One and His Ownhood," not because we are strongly impressed by the profundity of his thought but because we believe that here is a man who ought to be answered, whose world-conception deserves a careful analysis which finally would lead to a justification of society, the state and the ideals of right and truth.

Society is not, as Stirner imagines, an artificial product of men who band themselves together in order to produce a state for the benefit of a clique. Society and state, as well as their foundation the family, are of a natural growth. All the several social institutions (kind of spiritual organisms) are as much organisms as are plants and animals. The co-operation of the state with religious, legal, civic and other institutions, are as much realities as are individuals, and any one who would undertake to struggle against them or treat them as nonentities will be implicated in innumerable struggles.

Stirner is the philosopher of individualism. To him

the individual, this complicated and fluctuant being, is a reality, indeed the only true reality, while other combinations, institutions and social units are deemed to be mere nonentities. If from this standpoint the individualism of Stirner were revised, the student would come to radically different conclusions, and these conclusions would show that not without good reasons has the individual developed as a by-product of society, and all the possessions, intellectual as well as material, which exist are held by individuals only through the assistance and with the permission of the whole society or its dominant factors.

Both socialism and its opposite, individualism, which is ultimately the same as anarchism, are extremes that are based upon an erroneous interpretation of communal life. Socialists make society, and anarchists the individual their ultimate principle of human existence. Neither socialism nor anarchism are principles; both are factors, and both factors are needed for preserving the health of society as well as comprehending the nature of mankind. By neglecting either of these factors, we can only be led astray and arrive at wrong conclusions.

Poor Stirner wanted to exalt the ego, the sovereign individual, not only to the exclusion of a transcendent God and of the state or any other power, divine or social, but even to the exclusion of his own ideals, be it truth or anything spiritual; and yet he himself sacrificed his life for a propaganda of the ego as a unique and sovereign being. He died in misery and the recognition of his labors has slowly, very slowly, followed after his death. Yea, even after his death a rival individualist, Friedrich Nietzsche, stole his thunder and reaped the fame which Stirner had earned. Certainly this noble-minded, modest, altruistic egotist was paid in his own coin.

Did Stirner live up to his principle of ego sovereignty? In one sense he did; he recognized the right of every one to be himself, even when others infringed upon his own well-being. His wife fell out with him but he respected her sovereignty and justified her irregularities. Apparently he said to himself, "She has as much right to her own personality as I have to mine." But in another sense, so far as he himself was concerned, he did not. What became of his own rights, his ownhood, and the sweeping claim that the world was his property, that he was entitled to use or misuse the world and all mankind as he saw fit; that no other human being could expect recognition, nay not even on the basis of contracts, or promises, or for the sake of love, or humaneness and compassion? Did Stirner in his poverty ever act on the principle that he was the owner of the world, that there was no tie of morality binding on him, no principle which he had to respect? Nothing of the kind. He lived and died in peace with all the world, and the belief in the great ego sovereignty with its bold renunciation of all morality was a mere Platonic idea, a tame theory which had not the slightest influence upon his practical life.

Men of Stirner's type do not fare well in a world where the ego has come into its own. They will be trampled under foot, they will be bruised and starved, and they will die by the wayside. No, men of Stirner's type had better live in the protective shadow of a state; the worst and most despotic state will be better than none, for no state means mob rule or the tyranny of the bulldozer, the ruffian, the brutal and unprincipled self-seeker.

Here Friedrich Nietzsche comes in. Like Stirner, Nietzsche was a peaceful man; but unlike Stirner, Nietzsche had a hankering for power. Being pathological himself, without energy, without strength and without a healthy appetite and a good stomach, Nietzsche longed to play the part of a bulldozer among a herd of submissive human creatures whom he would control and command. This is Nietzsche's ideal, and he calls it the "overman." Here Nietzsche modified and added his own notion to Stirner's philosophy.

Individualistic philosophies are therefore based on an obvious error by misunderstanding the nature of the individual man, by forgetting the reality of society and its continued significance for the individual life. A careful investigation of the nature of the state as well as of our personality would have taught Stirner that both the state and the individual are realities. The state and society exist as much as the individuals of which they are composed,[1] and no individual can ignore in his maxims of life the rules of conduct, the moral principles, or whatever you may call that something which constitutes the conditions of his existence, of his physical and social surroundings. The dignity and divinity of personality does not exclude the significance of super-personalities; indeed, the two, superpersonal presences with their moral obligations and concrete human persons with their rights and duties, co-operate with each other and produce thereby all the higher values of life.

Stirner is onesided but, within the field of his onesided view, consistent. Nietzsche spurns consistency but accepts the field of notions created by Stirner, and, glorying in the same extreme individualism, proclaims the gospel of that individual who on the basis of Stirner's philosophy would make the best of a disorganized state of society, who by taking upon himself the functions of the state would utilize the advantages thus gained for the suppression of his fellow beings; and this kind of individual is dignified with the title "overman."

Nietzsche has been blamed for appropriating Stirner's thoughts and twisting them out of shape from the self-assertion of every ego consciousness into the autocracy of the unprincipled man of power; but we must concede that the common rules of literary ethics can not apply to individualists who deny all and any moral

[1] See the author's *The Nature of the State,* 1894, and *Personality,* 1911.

authority. Why should Nietzsche give credit to the author from whom he drew his inspiration if neither acknowledges any rule which he feels obliged to observe? Nietzsche uses Stirner as Stirner declares that it is the good right of every ego to use his fellows, and Nietzsche shows us what the result would be—the rise of a political boss, a brute in human shape, the overman.

Nietzsche is a poet, not a philosopher, not even a thinker, but as a poet he exercises a peculiar fascination upon many people who would never think of agreeing with him. Most admirers of Nietzsche belong to the class which Nietzsche calls the "herd animals," people who have no chance of ever asserting themselves, and become hungry for power as a sick man longs for health.

Individualism and anarchism continue to denounce the state, when they ought to reform it and improve its institutions. In the meantime the world wags on. The state exists, society exists, and innumerable social institutions exist. The individual grows under the influence of other individuals, his ideas—mere spooks of his brain—yet the factors of his life, right or wrong, guide him and determine his fate. There are as rare exceptions a few lawless societies in the wild West where a few outlaws meet by chance, revolver in hand, but even among them the state of anarchy does not last long, for by habit and precedent certain rules are established, and wherever man meets man, wherever they offer and accept one another's help, they co-operate or compete, they join hands or fight, they make contracts, form alliances, and establish rules, the result of which is society, the state, with all the institutions of the state, the administration, the legislature, the judiciary, with all the intricate machinery that regulates the interrelations of man to man.

The truth is that man develops into a rational, human and humane being through society by his intercourse with other men. Man is not really an individual in the sense of Stirner and Nietzsche, a being by himself and for himself, having no obligations to his fellows. Man is a part of the society through which he originated and to which he belongs and to overlook, to neglect and to ignore his relations to society, not to recognize definite obligations or rules of conduct which we formulate as duties is the grossest mistake philosophers can make, and this becomes obvious if we consider the nature of man as a social being as Aristotle has defined it.

ANOTHER NIETZSCHE

THE assertion of selfhood and the hankering after originality make Nietzsche the exponent of the absolute uniqueness of everything particular, and he goes to the extreme of denying all kinds of universality—even that of formal laws (the so-called uniformities of nature), reason, and especially its application in the field of practical life, morality. His ideal is "Be thyself! Be unique! Be original!" Properly speaking, we should not use the term ideal when speaking of Nietzsche's maxims of life, for the conception of an ideal is based upon a recognition of some kind of universality, and Nietzsche actually sneers at any one having ideals. The adherents of Nietzsche speak of their master as *"der Einzige,"* i. e., "the unique one," and yet (in spite of the truth that every thing particular is in its way unique) the uniformities of nature are so real and unfailing that Nietzsche is simply the representative of a type which according to the laws of history and mental evolution naturally and inevitably appears whenever the philosophy of nominalism reaches its climax. He would therefore not be unique even if he were the only one that aspires after a unique selfhood; but the fact is that there are a number of Nietzsches, he happening to be the best known of his type. Other advocates of selfhood, of course, will be different from Nietzsche in many unimportant details, but they will be alike in all points that are essential and characteristic. One of these Nietzsches is George Moore, a Britain who is scarcely familiar with the writings of his German double, but a few quotations from his book, *Confessions of a Young Man*, will show that he can utter thoughts which might have been written by Friedrich Nietzsche himself. George Moore says:

"I was not dissipated, but I loved the abnormal" (p. 18).

"I was a model young man indeed" (p. 20).

"I boasted of dissipations" (p. 19).

"I say again, let general principles be waived; it will suffice for the interest of these pages if it be understood that brain-instincts have always been, and still are, the initial and the determining powers of my being" (p. 47).

George Moore, like Nietzsche, is one of Schopenhauer's disciples who has become sick of pessimism. He says:

"That odious pessimism! How sick I am of it" (p. 310).

When George Moore speaks of God he thinks of him in the old-fashioned way as a big self, an individual and particular being. Hence he denies him. God is as dead as any pagan deity. George Moore says:

"To talk to us, the legitimate children of the nineteenth

century, of logical proofs of the existence of God, strikes us in just the same light as the logical proof of the existence of Jupiter Ammon" (p. 137).

George Moore is coarse in comparison with Nietzsche. Nietzsche is no cynic; he is pure-hearted and noble by nature. Moore is voluptuous and vulgar. Both are avowed immoralists, and if the principle of an unrestrained egotism be right, George Moore is as good as Nietzsche, and any criminal given to the most abominable vices would not be worse than either.

Nietzsche feels the decadence of the age and longs for health; but he attributes the cause of his own decadence to the Christian ideals of virtue, love, and sympathy with others. George Moore cherishes the same views; he says:

"We are now in a period of decadence, growing steadily more and more acute" (p. 239).

"Respectability . . . continues to exercise a meretricious and enervating influence on literature" (p. 240).

"Pity, that most vile of all vile virtues, has never been known to me. The great pagan world I love knew it not" (p. 200).

"The philanthropist is the Nero of modern times" (p. 185).

Both Nietzsche and Moore long for limitless freedom; but Moore seems more consistent, for he lacks the ideal of the overman and extends freedom to the sex relation, saying:

"Marriage—what an abomination! Love—yes, but not marriage . . . freedom limitless" (p. 168-169).

Moore loves art, but his view of art is cynical, and here too he is unlike Nietzsche; he says:

"Art is not nature. Art is nature digested. Art is a sublime excrement" (p. 178).

Both believe in the coming of a great social deluge. George Moore says:

"The French revolution will compare with the revolution that is to come, that must come, that is inevitable, as a puddle on the road-side compares with the sea. Men will hang like pears on every lamp-post, in every great quarter of London, there will be an electric guillotine that will decapitate the rich like hogs in Chicago" (p. 343).

Ideals are regarded as superstitions, and belief in ideas is deemed hypocritical. George Moore says:

"In my heart of hearts I think myself a cut above you, because I do not believe in leaving the world better than I found it; and you, exquisitely hypocritical reader, think that you are a cut above me because you say you would leave the world better than you found it" (p. 354).

The deeds of a man, his thoughts and aspirations, which constitute his spiritual self, count for nothing; the body alone is supposed to be real, and thus after death a pig is deemed more useful than a Socrates. Continues Moore:

"The pig that is being slaughtered as I write this line will leave the world better than it found it, but you will leave only a putrid carcass fit for nothing but the grave" (p. 353).

Wrong is idealized:

"Injustice we worship; all that lifts us out of the miseries of life is the sublime fruit of injustice.

"Man would not be man but for injustice" (p. 203).

"Again I say that all we deem sublime in the world's history are acts of injustice; and it is certain that if mankind does not relinquish at once and for ever, its vain, mad, and frantic dream of justice, the world will lapse into barbarism" (p. 205).

George Moore gives a moment's thought to the ideal of "a new art, based upon science, in opposition to the art of the old world that was based on imagination, an art that should explain all things and embrace modern life in its entirety, in its endless ramifications, be it, as it were, a new creed in a new civilization . . . that would continue to a more glorious and legitimate conclusion the work that the prophets have begun"; but he turns his back upon it. It would be after all a product of development; it would be the tyranny of a past age, and he says, "as well drink the dregs of yesterday's champagne" (p. 128).

NIETZSCHE'S DISCIPLES

IT is said that barking dogs do not bite, and this being true, we must look upon Nietzsche's philosophy as a harmless display of words and a burning desire for power without making any attempt to practice what he preached. His philosophy, so far as he is concerned, is a purely Platonic love of an unattainable star whose brilliance dazzled the imagination of a childlike peaceful weakling. Suppose, however, for argument's sake, that Nietzsche had been a man of robust health, and that he had been born at the time of great disturbances, offering unlimited chances to an unscrupulous ambition, would he under these circumstances have led the life he preached, and in case he had done so, would he have boldly and unreservedly admitted his principles while carrying out his plans? Did ever Cæsar or Napoleon or any usurper, such as Richard III, who unscrupulously aspired for power, own that he would shrink from nothing to attain his aim? Such a straightforward policy for any schemer would be the surest way of missing his aim. Such men, on the contrary, have played hypocrites, and have pretended to cherish ideals generally approved by the large masses of the people whom Nietzsche calls the herd. So it is obvious that the philosophy of Nietzsche if it were ever practically applied, would have become a secret doctrine known only to the initiated few, while the broad masses would be misguided by some demonstrative show of moral principles that might be pleasing to the multitudes and yet at the same time conceal the real tendency of the overman to gain possession of his superior position.

Nietzsche's influence upon professional philosophers is comparatively weak. Whenever mentioned by them, it is in criticism, and he is generally set aside as one-sided, and perhaps justly, because he was truly no philosopher in the strict sense of the word. He was no reasoner, no logician, and we can not, properly speaking, look upon his philosophy as a system or even a systematized view of the world. Nietzsche made himself the exponent of a tendency, and as such he has his followers among large masses of those very people whom he despised as belonging to the herds. As Nietzsche idealized this very quality in which he was lacking, so his followers recruit themselves from the ranks of those people who more than all others would be opposed to the rule of the overman. His most ardent followers are among the nihilists of Russia, the socialists and anarchists of all civilized countries. The secret reason of attraction, perhaps unknown to themselves, seems to be Nietzsche's defense of the blind impulse and the privilege which he claims for the overman to be himself in spite of law and order and morality, and also his contempt for rules, religious, philosophical, ethical or even logical, that would restrict the great sovereign passion for power.

Nietzsche's philosophy has taken a firm hold of a number of souls who rebel against the social, the political, the religious, and even the scientific, conditions of our civilization. Nietzsche is the philosopher of protest, and, strange to say, while he himself is aristocratic in his instincts, he appeals most powerfully to the masses of the people.

Nietzsche's disciples are not among the aristocrats, not among the scholars, not among the men of genius. His followers are among the people who believe in hatred and hail him as a prophet of the great deluge. His greatest admirers are anarchists, sometimes also socialists, and above all those geniuses who have failed to find recognition. Nietzsche's thought will prove veritable dynamite if it should happen to reach the masses of mankind, the disinherited, the uneducated, the proletariat, the Catilinary existences. Nietzsche's philosophy is an intoxicant to those whom he despised most; they see in him their liberator, and rejoice in his invectives.

Invectives naturally appeal to those who are as unthinking as the brutes of the field, but feel the sufferings of existence as much as do the beasts of burden.

They are impervious to argument, but being full of bitterness and envy they can be led most easily by any kind of denunciations of their betters. Nietzsche hated the masses, the crowd of the common people, the herd. He despised the lowly and had a contempt for the ideals of democracy. Nevertheless, his style of thought is such as to resemble the rant of the leaders of mobs, and it is quite probable that in the course of time he will become the philosopher of demagogues.

A great number of Nietzsche's disciples share their master's eccentricities and especially his impetuosity. Having a contempt for philosophy as the work of the intellect, they move mainly in the field of political and social self-assertion; they are anarchists who believe that the overman is coming in labor troubles, strikes, and through a subversion of the authority of government in any form.

The best known German expounders of Nietzsche's philosophy have been Rudolph Steiner and Alexander Tille.[1] Professor Henri Lichtenberger of the Univer-

[1] A. Tille, *Von Darwin bis Nietzsche.* R. Steiner, *Wahrheit und Wissenschaft; Die Philosophie der Freiheit;* and *F. Nietzsche, ein Kämpfer gegen seine Zeit.*

We have already mentioned the biography of Nietzsche published by the philosopher's sister, Frau E. Förster-Nietzsche. A characterization, disavowed by Nietzsche's admirers, was written by Frau Lou Andreas Salome, under the title *F. Nietzsche in seinen Werken.* Other works kindred in spirit are Schellwien's *Der Geist der neueren Philosophie,* 1895, and *Der Darwinismus,* 1896; also Adolf Gerecke, *Die Aussichtslosigkeit des Moralismus;* Schmitt, *An der Grenzscheide*

sity of Nancy was his interpreter in France,[2] and the former editor of *The Eagle and the Serpent*, known under the pseudonym of Erwin McCall, in England. This periodical, which flourished for a short time only, characterized its own tendency as follows:

> "*The Eagle and the Serpent* is a bi-monthly journal of egoistic philosophy and sociology which teaches that in social science altruism spells damnation and egoism spells salvation. In the war against their exploiters the exploited cannot hope to succeed till they act as a unit, an 'ego.'"

A reader of *The Eagle and the Serpent* humorously criticised the egoistic philosophy as follows:

> "DEAR EAGLE AND SERPENT,—I am one of those unreasonable persons who see no irreconcilable conflict between egoism and altruism. The altruism of Tolstoy is the shortest road to the egoism of Whitman. The unbounded love and compassion of Jesus made him conscious of being the son of God, and that he and the Father were one. Could egoism go further than this? I believe that true egoism and true altruism grow in precisely equal degree in the soul, and that the alleged qualities which bear either name and attempt to masquerade alone without their respective make-weights are shams and counterfeits. The real desideratum is balance, and that cannot be permanently preserved on one leg. However, you skate surprisingly well for the time being on one foot, and I have enjoyed the first performance so well that I enclose 60 cents for a season-ticket.—ERNEST H. CROSBY, RHINEBECK, N. Y., U. S. A.

A German periodical *Der Eigene*, i. e., "he who is

zweier Weltalter; Károly Krausz, *Nietzsche und seine Weltanschauung.*

[2] Henri Lichtenberger, *La philosophie de Nietzsche.* Paris, Alcan, 1898.

his own," announced itself as "a journal for all and nobody," and sounded "the slogan of the egoists," by calling on them to "preserve their ownhood."

Another anarchistic periodical that stood under the influence of Nietzsche appeared in Budapest,[3] Hungary, in German and Hungarian under the name *Ohne Staat,* ("Without Government") as "the organ of ideal anarchists," under the editorship of Karl Krausz.

Perhaps the most worthy exponent of Nietzsche in England today is his translator Thomas Common. He does not consider himself an orthodox Nietzsche apostle but thinks that Nietzsche has given the world a very important revelation and that his new philosophy of history and his explanation of the rôle of Christianity are among the most wonderful discoveries since

[3] We may mention incidentally that a contributor to *Ohne Staat* reproduced one of the Homilies of St. Chrysostom, in which he harangues after the fashion of the early Christian preachers against wealth and power. The state's attorney, not versed in Christian patristic literature, seized the issue and placed the man who quoted the old Byzantine saint behind the prison bars. In the issue of Nov., 1898, Dr. Eugen Heinrich Schmitt mentions the case and says: "Thus we have an exact and historical proof that the liberty of speech and thought was incomparably greater in miserable, servile Byzantium than it is now in the much more miserable and more servile despotism of modern Europe." Does not Dr. Schmitt overlook the fact that in the days of Byzantine Christianity the saints were protected by the mob, which was much feared by the imperial government and was kept at bay only by a nominal recognition of its claims and beliefs?

Darwin. At the same time Mr. Common pronounces Nietzsche's doctrine of eternal recurrence "very foolish" and believes his use of the terms "good" and "evil" so perverted that he was frequently confused about them and so misled superficial readers. Mr. Common published at regular intervals during the years 1903 to 1909 ten numbers of a small periodical entitled variously *Notes for Good Europeans* and *The Good European Point of View,* and expects to resume its publication soon. Its motto is from Nietzsche, "In a word—and it shall be an honorable word—we are Good Europeans . . . . the heirs of thousands of years of the European spirit." Its purpose is expressed in its first number as follows: "Our general purpose is to spread the best and most important knowledge relating to human well-being among those who are worthy to receive it, with a view to reducing the knowledge to practice, after some degree of unanimity has been attained. . . As Nietzsche's works, notwithstanding some limitations, exaggerations and minor errors, embody the foremost philosophical thought of the age, it will be one of our special objects to introduce these works to English readers."

These numbers contain many bibliographical and other notes of interest to friends or critics of the Nietzsche propaganda. Mr. Common has published selections from Nietzsche's works under the title, *Nietzsche as Critic, Philosopher, Poet and Prophet.*[4]

[4] Other recent English Nietzschean literature is as follows:

BUST OF NIETZSCHE, BY KLINGER

In America Nietzsche's philosophy is represented by a book of Ragnar Redbeard, entitled *Might is Right, the Survival of the Fittest.*[5] The author characterizes his work as follows:

"This book is a reasoned negation of the Ten Commandments—the Golden Rule—the Sermon on the Mount—Republican Principles—Christian Principles—and 'Principles' in general.

"It proclaims upon scientific evolutionary grounds, the unlimited absolutism of Might, and asserts that cut-and-dried moral codes are crude and immoral inventions, promotive of vice and vassalage."

The author is a most ardent admirer of Nietzsche, as may be learned from his verses made after the pattern of Nietzsche's poetry. He sings:

"There is no 'law' in heaven or earth that man must needs obey! Take what you can, and all you can; and take it while you—may.

"Let not the Jew-born Christ ideal unnerve you in the fight. You have no 'rights,' except the rights you win by—might.

"There is no justice, right, nor wrong; no truth, no good, no evil. There is no 'man's immortal soul,' no fiery, fearsome Devil.

"There is no 'heaven of glory:' No!—no 'hell where sin-

Grace Neal Dolson, *The Philosophy of Friedrich Nietzsche,* 1901; Oscar Levy, *The Revival of Aristocracy,* 1906; A. R. Orage, *Fried. Nietzsche, the Dionysian Spirit of the Age,* 1906; A. R. Orage, *Nietzsche in Outline and Alphorism;* Henry L. Mencken, *The Philosophy of Friedrich Nietzsche;* M. A. Mügge, *Friedrich Nietzsche: His Life and Work;* Anthony M. Ludovici, *Who Is to Be Master of the World?*

[5] Published by Adolph Mueller, Chicago.

ners roast.' There is no 'God the Father,' No!—no Son, no 'Holy Ghost.'

"This world is no Nirvâna where joy forever flows. It is a grewsome butcher shop where dead 'lambs' hang in—rows.

"Man is the most ferocious of all the beasts of prey. He rangeth round the mountains, to love, and feast, and—slay.

"He sails the stormy oceans, he gallops o'er the plains, and sucks the very marrow-bones of captives held in—chains.

"Death endeth all for every man,—for every 'son of thunder'; then be a lion (not a 'lamb') and—don't be trampled under."

A valuable recent addition to the discussion of egoism is *The Philosophy of Egoism* by James L. Walker, (Denver, 1905).

We know of no American periodical which stands for Nietzsche's views, except, perhaps, *The Lion's Paw* (Chicago) which claims to follow no one. In the last years of the nineteenth century Clarence L. Swartz published at Wellesley, Mass., an egoistic periodical called the *I*. This magazine is no longer in existence, but Mr. Swartz is very active in the International Intelligence Institute whose aims are universal language, universal nationality and universal peace. He still maintains the same philosophical view which he held as editor of the *I*, but his philosophical egoism has led him in far different paths from those of Nietzsche—into the paths of peace and not of struggle. He expresses his present conception as follows:

"In the last analysis there is no right but might. Such is the common ordinary rule of every-day life, from which there is no escape, even were escape desirable. Any attempt to overthrow or circumvent or even dispute the exercise of this prerogative of the mighty is but to assert or oppose a greater might. Expediency always dictates how might should be exercised. Politically, I hold that the non-coercion of the non-invasive individual is the part of wisdom. The individual is supreme, and should be preserved as against society, for in no other way can evolution perform its perfect work."

The Free Comrade edited by J. Wm. Lloyd and Leonard Abbott, an avowedly socialistic and individualistic paper, originally under the sole editorship of Lloyd, stood for Nietzsche and his egoism, but can no longer be said to do so.

THE PRINCIPLE OF VALUATION

IT may be interesting in this connection to mention the case of an American equivalent to Nietzsche's philosophy, which so far as I know has never yet seen publicity.

Some time ago the writer of this little book became acquainted with a journalist who has worked out for his own satisfaction a new system of philosophy which he calls "Christian economics," the tendency of which would be to preach a kind of secret doctrine for the initiated few who would be clever enough to avail themselves of the good opportunity. He claims that the only thing worth while in life is the acquisition of power through the instrumentality of money. He who acquires millions can direct the destiny of mankind, and this tendency was first realized in the history of mankind in this Christian nation of ours, whose ostensible faith is Christianity. Our religion, he argues, is especially adapted to serve as a foil to protect and conceal the real issue, and so he calls his world-conception, "Christian economics." Emperors and kings are mere puppets who are exhibited to general inspection, and so are presidents and all the magistrates in office. Political government has to obey the behests of the financiers, and the most vital life of mankind resides in its economical conditions.

The inventor of this new system of "Christian economics" would allow no other valuation except that of making money, on the sole ground that science, art and the pleasures of life are nothing to man unless he is in control of power which can be had only through the magic charm of the almighty dollar.

I shall not comment upon his view, but shall leave it to the reader, and am here satisfied to point out its similarity to Nietzsche's philosophy. There is one point only which I shall submit here for criticism and that is the principle of valuation which is a weak point with both the originator of "Christian economics" and with Friedrich Nietzsche.

Nietzsche proclaimed with great blast of trumpets, if we may so call his rhetorical display of phrases, that we need a revaluation of all values; but the best he could do was to establish a standard of valuation of his own. Every man in this world attains his mode of judging values according to his character, which is formed partly by inherited tendencies, partly by education and is modified by his own reflections and experiences. There are but few persons in this world who are clearsighted enough to formulate the ultimately guiding motive of their conduct. Most people follow their impulses blindly, but in all of them conduct forms a certain consistent system corresponding to their own idiosyncrasy. These impulses may sometimes be contradictory, yet upon the whole they will all agree, just as leaves and blossoms, roots and branches of the same tree will naturally be formed according to the secret plan that determines the growth of the whole organism. Those who work out a specially pronounced system of moral conduct do not always agree in practical life with their own moral principle, sometimes because they wilfully misrepresent it and more frequently because their maxims of morality are such as they themselves would like to be, while their conduct is such as they actually are. Such are the conditions of life and we will call that principle which as an ultimate *raison d'être* determines the conduct of man, his standard of valuation. We will see at once that there is a different standard for each particular character.

A scientist as a rule looks at the world through the spectacles of the scientist. His estimation of other people depends entirely on their accomplishments in his own line of science. Artist, musician, or sculptor does the same. To a professional painter scarcely any other people exist except his pupils, his master, his rivals and especially art patrons. The rest of the world is as indifferent as if it did not exist; it forms the background, an indiscriminate mass upon which all other values find their setting. All the professions and vocations, and all the workers along the various lines of life are alike in that every man has his own standard of valuation.

A Napoleon or a Cæsar might have preached the doctrine that the sciences, the arts and other accomplishments are of no value if compared with the acquisition of power, but I feel sure that it would not have been much heeded by the mass of mankind, for no one would change his standard of value. A financier might publicly declare that the only way to judge people is according to the credit they have in banking, but it would scarcely change the standard of judgment in society. Beethoven knew as well as any other of his contemporaries the value of money and the significance of power, and yet he pursued his own calling, fascinated by his love for music. The same is true not only of every genius in all the different lines of art and science, but also of religious reformers and inventors of all classes. Tom, Dick and Harry in their hankering for pleasure and frivolous amusement are not less under the influence of the conditions under which they have been born than the great men whose names are written in the book of fame. It is difficult for every one of us to create for himself a new standard of valuation, for what Goethe says of man's destiny in a poem entitled *Daimon*, is true:[1]

> "As on the day which has begotten thee
> The sun and planets stood in constellation,

[1] So far as I know, these lines have never been translated before.

> Thus growest and remainest thou to be,
> For 't is life's start lays down the regulation
> How thou must be. Thyself thou canst not flee.
> Such sibyl's is and prophet's proclamation.
> For truly, neither force nor time dissolveth,
> Organic form as, living, it evolveth."

The original reads thus:

> "Wie an dem Tag der dich der Welt verliehen,
> Die Sonne stand zum Grusse der Planeten,
> Bist alsobald and fort und fort gediehen
> Nach dem Gesetz, wonach du angetreten.
> So musst du sein, dir kannst du nicht entfliehen,
> So sagten schon Sibyllen, so Propheten;
> Und keine Zeit und keine Macht zerstückelt,
> Geprägte Form, die lebend sich entwickelt."

Our attitude in life depends upon our character, and the basic elements of character are the product of the circumstances that gave birth to our being. Our character enters unconsciously or consciously in the formulation of our standards of value which we will find to be the most significant factors of our destinies. Now the question arises, Is the standard of value which we set up, each one of us according to his character, purely subjective or is there any objective criterion of its worth?

We must understand that to a great extent our choice of a profession and other preferences in our occupations or valuations are naturally different according to conditions; some men are fit to be musicians, or scholars, or traders, or farmers, or manufacturers, and others are not. The same profession would not be appropriate for every one. But there is a field common to all occupations which deals with man's attitude toward his fellow beings and, in fact, toward the whole universe in general. This it is with which we are mainly concerned in our discussion of a criterion of value because it is the field occupied by religion, philosophy and ethics. Tradition has sanctioned definite views on this very subject which have been codified in certain rules of conduct different in many details in different countries according to religion, national and climatic conditions, and the type of civilization; yet, after all, they agree in most remarkable and surprising coincidences in all essential points.

Nietzsche, the most radical of radicals, sets up a standard of valuation of his own, placing it in the acquisition of power, and he claims that it alone is entitled to serve as a measure for judging worth because, says he, it alone deals with that which is real in the world; yet at the same time he disdains to recognize the existence of any objective criterion of the several standards of value. If he were consistent, he ought to give the palm of highest morality to the man who succeeds best in trampling under foot his fellowmen, and he does so by calling him the overman, but he does not call him moral. To be sure this would be a novel conception of morality and would sanction what is commonly execrated as one of the most devilish forms of immorality. Nietzsche takes morality in its accepted meaning, and so in contradiction to himself denies its justification in general.

Considering that every one carries a standard of valuation in himself we propose the question, "Is there no objective criterion of valuation, or are all valuations purely subjective?" This question means whether the constitution of the objective world in which we all live, is such as to favor a definite mode of action determined by some definite criterion of value.

We answer that subjective standards of valuation may be regarded as endorsed through experience by the course of events in the world whenever they meet with success, and thus subjective judgments become objectively justified. They are seen to be in agreement with the natural course of the world, and those who adhere to them will in the long run be rewarded by survival. Such an endorsement of standards can be determined by experience and has resulted in what is commonly called "morality." We may here take for granted that the moral valuation is a product of many millenniums and has been established, not only in one country and by one religion, nor in one kind of human society, but in perfect independence in many different countries, under the most varied conditions, and finds expression in the symbolism of the most divergent creeds. The beliefs of a Christian, of a Buddhist, of a Mussulman in Turkey, or a Taoist in the Celestial Empire, of a Parsee in Bombay, or a Japanese Shintoist, are all as unlike as they can be, but all agree as to the excellency of moral behavior which has been formulated in these different religions in sayings incorporated in their literature. We find very little if anything contradictory in their standards of valuation, and if there is any objective norm for the subjective valuation of man it is this moral consensus in which all the great religious prophets and reformers of mankind agree.

A transvaluation of all values is certainly needed, and it is taking place now. In fact it has always taken place whenever and wherever mankind grows or progresses or changes the current world-conception.

The old morality has been negative and we feel the need of positive ideals. The old doctrines are formulated in rules which forbid certain actions and our commandments begin with the words "Thou shalt not . . ." Those folk are esteemed moral who obey these restrictions or at least do not ostensibly infringe upon them, and this practically limits morality to mediocrity. How often have great and noble people been condemned as immoral because some irregularities would not fit the Procrustean bed of customary respectability! Think only of George Eliot who had to suffer under the prejudices of Sunday-School morality! We need a higher standard in which we may set aside the paltry views of the old morality without losing our ideals. We need a positive norm, the norm which counts in the actual world and in history, where man is measured not by his sins of omission but by his positive accomplishments; not by the errors he has or has not committed, but by his deeds, by the work with which he has benefited mankind. Therefore the new morality does not waste much time with the several injunctions, "Thou shalt not . . ." but impresses the growing generation with the demand: "Do something useful; show thyself efficient; be superior to others in nobility, in generosity, in energy; excel in one way or another"; and in this sense a transvaluation of the old values is being worked out at present.

We will grant that Nietzsche's demand of a transvaluation of all values may mean to criticize the narrow doctrines and views of the religion of his surroundings. But as he expresses himself and according to his philosophical principle he goes so far as to condemn not only the husk of all these religious movements, but also their spirit. In spite of his subjectivism which denies the existence of anything ideal, and goes so far as to deny the right even of truth to have an objective value, Nietzsche establishes a new objectivism, and proposes his own, and indeed very crude, subjective standard of valuation as the only objective one worthy of consideration for the transvaluation of all values.

Nietzsche's real world, or rather what he deemed to be the real world, is a dream, the dream of a sick man, to whom nothing possesses value save the boons denied him, physical health, strength, power to dare and to do.

The transvaluation of all values which Nietzsche so confidently prophesied, will not take place, at least not in the sense that Nietzsche believed. There is no reason to doubt that in the future as in the past history will follow the old conservative line of development in which different people according to their different characters will adopt their own subjective standards, and nature, by a survival of the fittest will select those for preservation who are most in agreement with this real world in which we live, a world from which Nietzsche, according to the sickly condition of his constitution, was separated by a wide gulf. He thirsted for it in vain, and we believe that he had a wrong conception of the wealth of its possibilities and viewpoints.

INDIVIDUALISM

NIETZSCHE is unquestionably a bold thinker, a Faust-like questioner, and a Titan among philosophers. He is a man who understands that the problem of all problems is the question, Is there an authority higher than myself? And having discarded belief in God, he finds no authority except pretensions.

Nietzsche apparently is only familiar with the sanctions of morality and the criterion of good and evil as they are represented in the institutions and thoughts established by history, and seeing how frequently they serve as tools in the hands of the crafty for the oppression of the unsophisticated masses of the people, he discards them as utterly worthless. Hence his truly magnificent wrath, his disgust, his contempt for underling man, for the masses, this muddy stream of present mankind.

If Nietzsche had dug deeper, he would have found that there is after all a deep significance in moral ideals, for there is an authority above the self by which the worth of the self must be measured. Truth is not a mere creature of the self, but is the comprehension of the immutable eternal laws of being which constitute the norm of existence. Our self, "that creating, willing, valuing 'I,' which (according to Nietzsche) is the measure and value of all things," is itself measured by that eternal norm of being, the existence of which Nietzsche does not recognize.

What is true of Nietzsche applies in all fundamental questions also to his predecessor, Max Stirner. It applies to individualism in any form if carried to its consistent and most extreme consequences.

Nietzsche is blind to the truth that there is a norm above the self, and that this norm is the source of duty and the object of religion; he therefore denies the very existence of duty, of conviction, of moral principles, of sympathy with the suffering, of authority in any shape, and yet he dares to condemn man in the shape of the present generation of mankind. What right has he, then, to judge the sovereign self of to-day and to announce the coming of another self in the overman? From the principles of his philosophical anarchism he has no right to denounce mankind of to-day, as an underling; for if there is no objective standard of worth, there is no sense in distinguishing between the underman of today and the overman of a nobler future.

On this point, however, Nietzsche deviates from his predecessor Stirner. The latter is more consistent as an individualist, but the former appeals strongly to the egoism of the individual.

Nietzsche is a Titan and he is truly Titanic in his rebellion against the smallness of everything that means to be an incarnation of what is great and noble and holy. But he does not protest against the smallness of the representatives of truth and right, he protests against truth and right themselves, and thus he is not merely Titanic, but a genuine Titan,—attempting to take the heavens by storm, a monster, not superhuman but inhuman in proportions, in sentiment and in spirit. Being ingenious, he is, in his way, a genius, but he is not evenly balanced; he is eccentric and, not recognizing the authority of reason and science, makes eccentricity his maxim. Thus his grandeur becomes grotesque.

The spirit of negation, the mischief-monger Mephistopheles, says of Faust with reference to his despair of reason and science:

> "Reason and Knowledge only thou despise,
> The highest strength in man that lies! . . .
> And I shall have thee fast and sure."
> —*Tr. by Bayard Taylor.*

Being giant-like, the Titan Nietzsche has a sense only for things of large dimensions. He fails to understand the significance of the subtler relations of existence. He is clumsy like Gargantua; he is coarse in his reasoning; he is narrow in his comprehension; his horizon is limited. He sees only the massive effects of the great dynamical changes brought about by brute force; he is blind to the quiet and slow but more powerful workings of spiritual forces. The molecular forces that are invisible to the eye transform the world more thoroughly than hurricanes and thunderstorms; yet the strongest powers are the moral laws, the curses of wrong-doing and oppression, and the blessings of truthfulness, of justice, of good-will. Nietzsche sees them not; he ignores them. He measures the worth of the overman solely by his brute force.

If Nietzsche were right, the overman of the future who is going to take possession of the earth will not be nobler and better, wiser and juster than the present man, but more gory, more tiger-like, more relentless, more brutal.

Nietzsche has a truly noble longing for the advent of the overman, but he throws down the ladder on which man has been climbing up, and thus losing his foothold, he falls down to the place whence mankind started several millenniums ago.

We enjoy the rockets of Nietzsche's genius, we understand his Faust-like disappointment as to the unavailableness of science such as he knew it; we sympathize with the honesty with which he offered his thoughts to the world; we recognize the flashes of truth which occur in his sentences, uttered in the tone of a prophet; but we cannot help condemning his philosophy as unsound in its basis, his errors being the result of an immaturity of comprehension.

Nietzsche has touched upon the problem of problems, but he has not solved it. He weighs the souls of his fellowmen and finds them wanting; but his own soul is not less deficient. His philosophy is well worth studying, but it is not a good guide through life. It is great only as being the gravest error, boldly, conscientiously, and seriously carried to its utmost extremes and preached as the latest word of wisdom.

It has been customary that man should justify himself before the tribunal of morality, but Nietzsche summons morality itself before his tribunal. Morality justifies herself by calling on truth, but the testimony of truth is ruled out, for truth—objective truth—is denounced as a superstition of the dark ages. Nietzsche knows truth only as a contemptible method of puny spirits to make existence conceivable—a hopeless task! Nietzsche therefore finds morality guilty as a usurper and a tyrant, and he exhorts all *esprits forts* to shake off the yoke.

We grant that the self should not be the slave of morality; it should not feel the "ought" as a command; it should identify itself with it and make its requirements the object of its own free will. Good-will on earth will render the law redundant; but when you wipe out the ideal of good-will itself together with its foundation, which is truth and the recognition of truth, the struggle for existence will reappear in its primitive fierceness, and mankind will return to the age of savagery. Let the *esprits forts* of Nietzsche's type try to realize their master's ideal, and their attempts will soon lead to their own perdition.

We read in *Der arme Teufel,*[1] a weekly whose radical editor would not have been prevented by conventional reasons from joining the new fad of Nietzscheanism, the following satirical comment on some modern poet of original selfhood:

"'I am against matrimony because I am a poet. Wife, children, family life,—well, well! they may be good enough for the man possessed of the herding instinct. But I object to trivialities in my own life. I want something stimulating, sensation, poetry! A wife would be prosaic to me, simply on account of being my wife; and children who would call me papa would be disgusting. Poetry I need! Poetry!' Thus he spoke to a friend, and when the latter was gone continued his letter reproaching a waitress for again asking for money and at the same time reflecting upon the purity of her relations to the bartender who, she pretended, was her cousin only. . . ."

If marriage relations were abolished to-day, would not in the course of time some new form of marriage be established? Those who are too proud to utilize the experiences of past generations, will have to repeat them for themselves and must wade through their follies, sins, errors, and suffer all the consequences and undergo their penalties.

Nietzsche tries to produce a Cæsar by teaching his followers to imitate the vices of a Catiline; he would raise gods by begetting Titans; he endeavors to give a nobler and better standard to mankind, not by lifting

[1] May 13, 1899. Detroit, 949 Gratiot Ave.

the people higher and rendering them more efficient, but by depriving them of all wisdom and making them more pretentious.

If the ethics of Nietzsche were accepted to-day as authoritative, and if people at large acted accordingly, the world would be benefited in one respect, viz., hypocrisy would cease, and the selfishness of mankind would manifest itself in all its nude bestiality. Passions would have full sway; lust, robbery, jealousy, murder, and revenge would increase, and Death in all forms of wild outbursts would reap a richer harvest than he ever did in the days of prehistoric savage life. The result would be a pruning on a grand scale, and after a few bloody decades those only would survive who either by nature or by hypocritical self-control deemed it best to keep the lower passions and the too prurient instincts of their selfhood in proper check, and then the old-fashioned rules of morality, which Nietzsche declared antiquated, would be given a new trial in the new order of things. They might receive a different sanction, but they would find recognition.

Nietzsche forgets that the present social order originated from that general free-for-all fight which he commends, and that if we begin at the start we should naturally run through the same or a similar course of development to the same or very similar conditions. Will it not be better to go on improving than to revert to the primitive state of savagery?

There are superstitious notions about the nature of

the sanction of ethics, but for that reason the moral ideals of mankind remain as firmly established as ever.

The self is not the standard of measurement for good and evil, right and wrong, as Nietzsche claims in agreement with the sophists of old; the self is only the condition to which and under which it applies. There is no good and evil in the purely physical world, there is no suffering, no pain, no anguish—all this originates with the rise of organized animal life which is endowed with sentiency; and further there is no goodness and badness, no morality until the animal rises to the height of comprehending the nature of evil. The tiger is in himself neither good nor bad, but he makes himself a cause of suffering to others; and thus he is by them regarded as bad. Goodness and badness are relative, but they are not for that reason unreal.

It is true that there is no "ought" in the world as an "ought"; nor are there metaphysical ghosts of divine commandments revealing themselves. But man learns the lesson how to avoid evil and reducing it to brief rules which are easily remembered, he calls them "commandments."

Buddha was aware that there is no metaphysical ghost of an "ought," and being the first positivist before positivism was ever thought of, his decalogue is officially called "avoiding the ten evils," not "the ten commandments," the latter being a popular term of later origin.

Granting that there is no metaphysical "ought" in

the world and that it finds application only in the domain of animate life through the presence of the self or rather of many selves, we fail to see that the self is the creator of the norm of good and evil. Granting also that there are degrees of comprehending the nature of evil and that different applications naturally result under different conditions, we cannot for that reason argue that ethics are purely subjective and that there is no objective norm that underlies the moral evolution of mankind and comes out in the progress of civilization more and more in its purity.

Nietzsche is like a schoolboy whose teacher is an inefficient pedant. He rebels against his authority and having had but poor instruction proclaims that the multiplication table is a mere superstition with which the old man tries to enslave the free minds of his scholars. Are there not different solutions possible of the same example and has not every one to regard his own solution as the right solution? How can the teacher claim that he is the standard of truth? Why, the very attempt at setting up a standard of any kind is tyranny and the recognition of it is a self-imposed slavery. There is no rightness save the rightness that can be maintained in a general hand-to-hand contest, for it is ultimately the fist that decides all controversies.

Nietzsche calls himself an atheist; he denies the existence of God in any form, and thus carries atheism to an extreme where it breaks down in self-contradiction. We understand by God (whether personal, impersonal, or superpersonal) that something which determines the course of life; the factors that shape the world, including ourselves; the law to which we must adjust our conduct. Nietzsche enthrones the self in the place of God, but for all practical purposes his God is blunt success and survival of the fittest in the crude sense of the term; for according to his philosophy the self must heed survival in the struggle for existence alone, and that, therefore, is his God.

Nietzsche's God is power, i. e., overwhelming force, which allows the wolf to eat the lamb. He ignores the power of the still small voice, the effectiveness of law in the world which makes it possible that man, the over-brute, is not the most ferocious, the most muscular, or the strongest animal. Nietzsche regards the cosmic order, in accommodation to which ethical codes have been invented, as a mere superstition. Thus it will come to pass that Nietzsche's type of the overman, should it really make its appearance on earth, would be wiped out as surely as the lion, the king of the beasts, the proud pseudo-overbrute of the animals, will be exterminated in course of time. The lion has a chance for survival only behind the bars of the zoölogical gardens or when he allows himself to be tamed by man, that weakling among the brutes whose power has been built up by a comprehension of the sway of the invisible laws of life, physical, mental and moral.

What is the secret of Nietzsche's success? While other men of greater consistency, among them his predecessor Stirner, failed, he attained an unparalleled fame, and his philosophy exercised an extraordinary influence upon large classes of people not only in Germany but also abroad, in Russia, in France, in the United States and even in conservative England.

We must concede that Nietzsche possesses a poetic power of oratory; he appeals to sentiment; he is not much of a thinker, not a philosopher, but a leader and a prophet, and as such he stands for the most extreme egoism. Nietzsche attempts to establish the absolute sovereignty of the individual and grants a most irresponsible freedom to the man who dares; and this principle of doing away with moral maxims has made him popular.

The truth is that our moral sanctions are no longer accepted. People still believe in God, in the authority of church and state, but their belief is no longer a living faith. Whatever they may think of God, the old God, the God of traditional dogmatism, is gone. He is no longer a living power in the hearts of the people; and so, large masses rejoice to have the proclamation frankly stated that God is dead, that they need no longer fear hell, and that the chains of their slavery are broken.

Nietzsche is consistent in his denial of the traditional sanctions. He understands not only that there are no gods, that the powers of nature as personifications do not exist, but that the laws of nature are mere abstract generalizations. We need no longer believe in Hephaestos, the god of fire; there is no use to bow the knee to him or do homage to his divinity. Nor is there any truth in the existence of a phlogiston, a metaphysical fire-stuff, or any fire essence; there are only scattered facts of burning. Everything else is mere superstition. Generalizations exist only in our imagination, and so we should get rid of the idea that there is any truth at all. Science is a pretender which is apt to make cowards of us. That man is wise who is not hampered by scruple or doubt of any kind and simply follows the bent of his mind, subjecting to himself every thing he finds, including his fellow human beings.

This bold and reckless proposition appeals to egoism and it seems so true that abstract formulas and generalizations are empty. Weight exists; there is gravity; there are particular phenomena of masses in mutual attraction, but gravitation, the law of these actual happenings, is a mere formula, an imaginary quantity, a mere thought about which we need not worry. The law of gravitation is a human invention and has no real existence in the realm of facts.

And the same would of course be true about the interrelations among human beings in their social intercourse, too. All the several maxims of conduct, which are called moral and constitute our code of ethics, are built upon generalizations. There is no sanction for them. The gods who were formerly supposed to be responsible for the several domains of facts have died long ago. The Jewish deity called Elohim, the Lord, entered upon the inheritance of the ancient gods, but he too had to die. Thereupon his place was taken by metaphysical essences, pale ghosts of a mysterious nature, but they too died and so the last shadow of anything authoritative is gone. We are *en face du rien;* therefore let us boldly enjoy our freedom. Let us be ourselves; let our passions take their course; let us do wrong if it suits us; let us live without consideration of anything, just as we please. There is no sanction of moral maxims to be respected; there is no authority of conduct; there is no judge; there is no evil, no wrong.

This seems pretty plausible to our modern generation raised in the traditions of nominalism, but would we really ignore the law of gravitation because the Newtonian formula is a man-made abstraction and a mere generalization? Yet, if we do not give heed to it we fall, and the same is true of any law of nature. Our sciences are mental constructions; they are mind-made, and so far as they are built out of the material of our experience they tally with facts and we call them true. Our social interrelations, too, constitute conditions observable in experience; they can be formulated in laws and applied to practical life; they can be expressed in maxims of conduct and have received various sanctions successively, the sanctions of religion, the sanctions of metaphysics, the sanctions of science. In the age of savagery the sanction of moral maxims was offered us in a mythological dress. With the rise of monotheism our moral sanction came to us as the command of a supreme ruler of the universe; in the age of abstract philosophy as metaphysical principles, and in the age of science these should be recognized as lessons of experience.

CONCLUSION.

WE will gladly grant that personifications are mythological fictions, that metaphysical entities are products of a philosophical imagination and that the scientific formulas are abstract generalizations, but we deny that generalizations are unmeaning; they signify some actual features of reality. Abstract ideas are not purely fictitious; they denote significant qualities or occurrences, and the relations in life, the forms of things, combinations, or in general the non-material configurations, co-operations, combinations and functions are the most important and the most significant aspects of existence. Indeed, matter and energy are only the clumsy conditions of being; they denote actuality and reality, but all things, all events, all facts are such as they are on account of their form—on account of that feature which is non-material and non-energetic.

According to Nietzsche the whole history of mankind, especially the development of reason, knowledge and science, is a great blunder, and the dawn of day begins with a radical break with the past. We see in the evolution of life a gradual ascent with a slow but constant approximation to truth. In the history of religion we see in the dawn of civilization the beginning of a comprehension of truth. Mythology is not error pure and simple, not a conglomeration of superstitions; it is plainly characterized by a groping after great truths, and myths become foolish inventions only when the poetic character of the tale is misunderstood. So dogmas become dangerous errors when the symbol is taken literally, when the letter is exalted and the spirit forgotten. It is true that science has taken away the charm of many religious beliefs, but the great lesson of the doctrine of evolution is to show us that our onward march in the humanization of man does not stop, that the periods of mythology and dogma are stages in the progress of our recognition of the truth. There is no need to fear a collapse of past results but we may boldly build higher. We must search for truth and we shall have a clearer vision of it, and the future will bring new glories, new fulfilments of old hopes and grander realization of our fondest dreams.

Verily, the overman will come, although he is not quite so near at hand as one might wish. He is at hand though, but he will not come, as Nietzsche announces him, in the storm of a catastrophe. The fire and the storm may precede the realization of a higher humanity; but the higher humanity will be found neither in the fire nor in the storm. The overman will be born of the present man, not by a contempt for the shortcomings of the present man, but by a recognition of the essential features of man's manhood, by developing and purifying the truly human by making man conform to the eternal norm of rationality, humaneness and rightness of conduct.

What we need first is the standard of the higher man; and on this account we must purify our notions of the norm of truth and righteousness,—of God. Let us find first the over-God, and the overman will develop naturally. The belief in an individual God-being is giving way to the recognition of a superpersonal God, the norm of scientific truth, the standard of right and wrong, the standard of worth by which we measure the value of our own being; and the kingdom of the genuine overman will be established by the spread of the scientific comprehension of the world, in matters physical, social, intellectual, moral, and religious.

*

*   *

INDEX

INDEX

INDEX

INDEX

INDEX

INDEX